CBT Workbook for Kids

Strategies and Exercises to Help Children Overcome Their Emotional Disorders and Fears. The Best Activities to Help Kids Deal with Anxiety, Stress, Anger and Adhd.

RACHEL DAVIDSON MILLER

as a result of the use of the information contained within this document, including, but not limited to, errors, omissions, or inaccuracies.

TABLE OF CONTENTS

Introduction

It is challenging to accept or even understand how a young child can feel big emotions like anxiety, stress, depression, and uncontrollable anger. Parents do everything they can to protect their children from situations and events that can cause their child to feel unsafe or unhappy. Despite your best efforts, your child may be secretly suffering and trying to tell you what is going on. The way children communicate these big and distressing emotions is often through inappropriate or harmful behavior.

Children lack a number of skills that can help them work through intense emotions. When these emotions are neglected or ignored, it can lead to serious conditions that can be even more challenging for the child to work through. While parents can do their best to cheer their child up and try to correct unwanted behavior, without understanding the root cause, your child will never overcome what is troubling them.

Cognitive Behavioral Therapy (CBT) is a highly effective form of therapy that is used with children, teens, and adults. This type of therapy establishes specific goals and provides valuable tools and techniques that can help children of any age work through challenging behaviors, thoughts, and emotions.

Unlike many other forms of therapy, CBT focuses on helping patients understand the connections among their thoughts, emotions, and behaviors. By realizing and becoming aware of how each of these elements affects and can impact the other, children can begin to identify what their triggers are.

Parents are an essential component for CBT to be effective. Parents will need to assist the therapy by supporting the practice of the techniques and by teaching their child the skills they may be lacking to help them gain control over their emotions, thoughts, and behaviors. With the encouragement of the parents and the support of a therapist, children can learn to successfully overcome big emotions.

This book will provide you with the information necessary to understand what your child may be struggling with. It will walk you through the process of CBT assessment and goal setting. You will learn how to identify troubling behaviors at home and at school and how you can react to your child when they are struggling. You will find exercises at the end of each chapter to do with your child. There are also additional exercises and tips that you and your child can do together to strengthen their emotional toolbox, increase self-esteem, and set them up for success for the rest of their life.

Chapter 1: What Is Cognitive Behavioral Therapy?

Cognitive Behavioral Therapy is a form of psychotherapy and talk therapy. It focuses on teaching individuals of any age how to deal with their emotions, thoughts, and change behaviors.

What Is CBT for?

CBT is used with children, teens, and adults to show them how to change negative thinking patterns, have a more positive view of themselves and the world around them, and show them how their thoughts, emotions, and behaviors are connected.

Together, the therapist and child, create specific goals that will provide the child with tools to manage their emotions, have more positive thoughts, and control their behaviors.

Who Can CBT Benefit?

CBT can be highly beneficial for many children who struggle with various forms of behavioral issues like impulse control. It can also allow those who may be lagging behind in their learning or developmental abilities. Children who have learning disabilities or challenges will suffer more from low self-esteem, negative thoughts, and emotional control.

CBT can help children cope with the way they are treated by others because of their differences. It allows them to learn skills that will give them confidence and control.

What can CBT help with?

CBT can help children that suffer from:

- Anxiety
- Depression
- Stress
- Anger
- Trauma
- ADHD

Children do not need to have a disorder to take part in CBT. CBT is highly beneficial in showing children at a young age that they can stop, rewire their thinking, and react appropriately to the challenges they face. Your child may be struggling with low self-esteem, social anxiety, emotional regulation, and many other obstacles that are not medically diagnosed. CBT can help you and your child work through these obstacles and will ensure that they have the proper skills to handle more challenging situations as they get older.

Chapter 2: How a Cognitive Behavioral Path Is Structured

Getting your child the help they need may require you to answer a vast number of questions. Though getting your child assessed for CBT can be a little time consuming it is crucial to understand that the information gathered will help you and your child uncover the core problem. Once the problem has been identified, you can establish goals and create an action plan to help your child overcome the problem.

What Are Your Child's Difficulties?

Your child will go through a number of assessments to determine where and what they are specifically struggling with. These assessments are non-intrusive and primarily include a number of different questions that your child, you, teachers, and others involved in your child's life may answer. The question asked will help uncover the problems and address the triggers, history, and additional factors that cause the problem to continue to occur.

Dialogue assessment

An initial assessment will begin with the therapist speaking to you and your child. During this time the therapist will ask a number of questions to uncover the core problem your child may be struggling with. They may use toys or ask them to draw out pictures of some of the things they feel or do. These questions will typically revolve around:

12

- What the internal thoughts are of the child.
- What behaviors the child exhibits.
- How the child feels about themselves, the people around them, and how they view the world or specific situation.
- When the problem started.
- How intense the problem is when it occurs.

This initial dialogue gives the therapist a general idea if your child is a good candidate for CBT and they will discuss with you the steps of the process.

Testing

Various testing is done to help uncover any underlying conditions your child may have. Testing can focus on:

- Your child's overall health
- Their fine motor skills
- How well they read and write
- The level of learning they possess and if it at the appropriate level for their age (can they count to ten, identify letters of the alphabet, know sight words, etc.)
- Social skills
- Their family dynamic
- Emotional regulation or their level of understanding of emotions

These tests are done in a neutral environment where the child will not feel pressured to perform.

Parent/Caregiver questionnaires

Parents will be given a questionnaire that will give the therapist or team of therapist an overview of concerns you may have. While these questionnaires can be lengthy and cover a range of concerns that address your child's thoughts, emotions, and behaviors, the overall goal is to clearly define what the main concerns are. Assessments for parents will ask you to:

- Identify your concerns, or struggles you are having with your child or notice your child is having.
- Uncover any links between the problem and situation factors. Are there themes, such as rules imposed on the child they are unable to follow or beliefs the child may have that need to be addressed?
- What the links are between your child's emotions, thoughts, or behaviors in a given situation.
- Are there certain people, places, or environmental factors that contribute to the problem?
- What helps resolve the problem?
- What causes the problem to intensify?
- What is the history of the problem? How long has it been occurring?
- When did the behavior start?
- How has the problem progressed since you first noticed it? Has it become more frequent? More intense?
- Is there any history of the problem that predisposed the child, such as family history, troubles in schools? Is there anything that could have triggered the problem to start?

14

- What causes the problem to persist?

- Who does your child interact with the most? (List family, child care, teachers, peers, and others who are significant people in your child's life.)

- How do the other people in your child's life address the problem?

- What strengths does your child possess?

- What are your family strengths?

- What strengths does your child's school/teachers/childcare offer?

- How motivated is your child to change the problem?

- How much support can the family give in helping change the problem?

- How can your child's school/teachers/child care support in helping change the problem?

- What other support do you have in helping address and change the problem?

- What have you tried in the past to help resolve this problem?

- Why do you and your child think the problem has been unable to resolve in the past?

- What do you and your child think can be helpful in solving this problem now?

You may have more than one concern or problem you would like to have help with solving. You will want to answer each of these questions for each of the problems. Additional question you can expect cover your pregnancy and your child's development.

Teacher questionnaires

If your child attends school, the teacher can fill out a simple questionnaire that will identify issues your child may be having outside the home. Teachers will answer the questions to better assess your child social skills, education achievements, and their ability to follow directions and finish a task. Teacher assessment can also uncover issues your child may be having with transition, understanding material, or learning difficulties and behavioral problems not present in the home setting.

Many questions teachers answer are similar to the ones you will answer as a parent but will focus primarily on the school setting and the skills they already possess. Some of these questions can include:

- Does the child appear happy?
- Does the child play appropriately with peers?
- Does the child have an understanding of material that is appropriate for their age?
- Does the child struggle to sit still?
- Does the child seem to be anxious? If so when is this noticeable?

Often teachers are given specific questionnaires that address what the main problem might be. For instance, if you suspect your child has ADHD, the teacher will be given a questionnaire that is heavily geared towards confirming a diagnosis. If your child has anxiety the questionnaire provided will more focused toward understanding what triggers the anxiety throughout the day.

Once the questionnaire and general assessments have been conducted and reviewed, you will begin to address the core problems that have been uncovered or already discussed. There are often specific areas your child will need help with. The areas your child may need help controlling include:

- Self-defeating thoughts
- Impulse control
- Defiance
- Emotional outbursts or tantrums
- Negative self-talk
- Self-control

Your child may also need help learning new coping mechanisms, problem-solving skills, or how to improve their self-image.

Establishing Goals

CBT is goal-oriented. If your child is approved for CBT, the therapist will work with you and your child to set a specific goal that involves overcoming or changing the problem. When establishing the goal, you will consider:

1. What is the core problem your child is having?
2. How would solving this problem impact your child and the other people involved in your child's life?
3. Can you and your child agree on the goal?

The established goal will be specific and address one problem at a time. This goal will have a measurable time frame, meaning it can be achieved in a realistic and short amount of time. The goal that is agreed upon will be one the child can achieve. Sometimes very short-term goals will be established in order to build your child's confidence so that they learn quickly that they do have the power to change their behavior, thoughts, and/or gain control over their emotions.

Achieving goals

Once a goal has been established, an action plan will be created to move your child forward quickly to achieving this goal. You can help establish goals by following these easy steps:

1. What is the goal?

You want to have a clearly defined goal to begin with. This is a simple step where you ask what it is that you want to achieve. You and your child should agree on the goal set and have an understanding of why this goal is important for the both of you.

2. Where are you starting?

Once you have set a clear goal you want to be honest about where it is your child is starting. What skills does your child have already and what skills do they need to improve? If your child has significant anger issues, than your starting point may include the negative impact their anger has on themselves and others. Look closely at how the problem is affecting the home life, family dynamics, and school. This may not be easy to do and can be disheartening for some parents and the child. But, keep in mind that where you are starting at now is just that: a starting point. Maintain a positive attitude and outlook that it is possible to change where you are starting from. Being honest about where you are starting allows you to clearly see where progress can be made. Looking at things in this manner and reassuring your child that change is possible, encourages them to put in the effort to work towards their goal.

3. What steps need to be taken?

Now that you know where you are starting, you can map out the steps that need to be taken to get your child where they want to go. Each goal you establish will involve taking small steps. Rarely is a goal achieved in just one step. Break down the goals in a way that will make it easily achievable for your child. Think of all the things that will need to be addressed and changed in order for your child to have success. Each step that is achieved will build your child's confidence so though they may be slightly challenged, you still want to ensure that your child is able to accomplish each step.

4. What is the first step you need to take?

Once you have the steps written out you need to put them in order. Think of what needs to be done in order to reach the end goal. Define what the first step to take will be and then ask what the next step needs to be. Some of the most common first steps for your child to take include:

- Learning the different emotions
- Understanding how emotions feel in the body

- Identifying situations where they feel anxious, afraid, sad, or angry
- Understanding how their emotions or behaviors affect others
- Putting themselves in another person's shoes
- Understanding what thoughts are
- Being able to spot negative and positive thoughts

These first steps seem simple, but many children lack the understanding of many of these basic first steps. This lack of basic understanding can often be the root cause of the problem they are having. Once you have established the first step, move on to outline the next step, and so on.

5. What obstacles might stand in your way when you take this first step.

Each step is bound to have certain obstacles that your child will need to learn and overcome. Many times it is our thoughts that stand in the way of making it possible to achieve a certain goal. Maybe your child does not think they are smart enough to learn what they need to learn to achieve the goal. This is an obstacle that will involve supplying your child with positive thoughts that will help them move forward. You will learn more about how to change negative thoughts to positive ones later in this book. For now, simply ask your child what they think may keep them from accomplishing each step. When you have all the potential obstacles laid out, you can learn how to work through them.

6. How will you take the first step?

Now that you have established the goal, outlined action steps, and have considered potential obstacles, it is time to get started. When it comes to getting started, first think about how much time you are going to commit to working on that step each day. Children may not be able to work on action steps for long periods of time but there are many ways you can work on goals throughout the day to get to the end result faster. For instance, if you know your child needs to improve their understanding of basic emotions you can sit down and work on the different emotions with them. You can also incorporate identifying emotions when you read to them, when they are watching their favorite television show, or by talking with them about your day and theirs. You can simply ask them how a character felt when something happened to them, or you can ask them how they think a character feels based on their facial expression and body language. This allows you plenty of opportunities to work toward that first step in a fun and less stressful way.

If you are participating in a CBT session, the therapist will often begin by speaking to your child about the problem and ask for examples and details about when the problem occurs. Then, the therapist will provide tools and address specific areas that are contributing to the problem. These tools will be practiced through role-playing, so you and your child understand how to implement them in daily life. At the end of the session, a homework assignment is typically given to encourage your child to utilize what was covered during the session.

Therapy tools

- **Play** - The therapist will use role-play to help your child understand and use tools to work through a difficult problem. You can do this at home as well. If you know your child had a hard time that day you can ask them to use their toys to replay what occurred. You can then ask them what they could have done differently and how that could have affected the outcome of the situation.

- **Drawing** - Drawing can be utilized to help your child overcome any emotions or behavioral problems. It is also a great way to help them identify negative thoughts. Throughout this book, you will find various exercises that involve drawing to help work through specific problems and to strengthen their skills.

- **Dialog** - How you speak to your child will have a significant impact on their ability to understand and use the tools discussed. Creating a clear path of communication between you and your child is essential for their success. The therapist will go over phrases to use with your child to better encourage and assist them. There is a chapter later in this book that specifically covers how to encourage and open the lines of communication between you and your child.

- **Social Stories** - Social stories can be an effective way to help your child understand challenging topics. Social stories are created to allow your child to identify themselves in specific situations. These stories will place your child as the main character and will describe how they act, think, and the emotions they may be feeling in certain situations. They also address problem-solving techniques and tools your child can use when they are in that situation.

- **Games** - Games are an easy way to teach children basic skills like patience, being a good sport, and problem-solving. You can make time to play any number of games with your child, which will also provide you with one-on-one bonding time. In the last chapter of this book you will find a list of games that are ideal for helping your child identity emotions, practice impulse control, promote communication, and much more. You can easily convert some games you probably have at home into "therapy" games, which you will learn more about later.

CBT utilizes a wide range of simple and effective tools that will help your child reach the desired goal. These tools can be used at home, in school, or in the community. They need to be practiced regularly to ensure that your child can fully understand how and when to use the techniques learned through these tools in everyday situations. The more you practice with your child the more they develop and strengthen these techniques.

The Goal of CBT

Though you will establish a specific goal to work towards, each will focus on the CBT basics discussed in the previous chapter. The tools used through CBT will provide your child with the abilities to:

- Understand negative thoughts
- Recognize emotions

- Make a connection between thoughts, emotions, and behaviors

Each goal established will focus on one of these three aspects:

Evaluating the results:

Once you have begun taking the first steps to reach the goal you will want to evaluate the progress after each step. This will allow you and your child to agree on what may have worked and what still needs to improve. You will also be able to brainstorm different ways to achieve each step. With each step, you should keep track of the tools that were used and how effective they were. You can track your findings in a simply way outlined below.

What are the advantages?

- What tool was used?

- How did this tool help in achieving the goal?

- How often was the tool used by your child in an everyday setting?

- Has this tool helped your child gain a better understanding of their emotions, thoughts, or behaviors?

- What situation did this tool help with?

- How else can this tool be used to assist your child?

What are the disadvantages?

- How difficult was it for your child to use this tool?

- How challenging was it for your child to understand why this tool is beneficial?

- Did this tool make it more challenging for your child to understand or control their thoughts, feelings, or behaviors?

- Why was this tool difficult for your child to use?

- Can this tool be modified to better help your child?

If your child has made a consistent effort to use the tool to help them but did not have success with the tool, then it might not be the right one for them. If your child was inconsistent in using the tool, then you need to address why it was difficult for your child to use this tool and in what situations it was not helpful. From here you can better understand what may help your child more as they move closer to the goals. For example, some children do really well when they have visual cues to remind them how to use the tool, other children need more role-playing, so they become more comfortable knowing when to use the tools. Each child is different and by keeping track of what is and isn't working you will be able to find the right tools the help your child be more successful.

Chapter 3: Anxiety

Anxiety is what helps us avoid dangerous situations and think about our behaviors. It is the natural way we protect ourselves. We often think of anxiety being an adult condition that can affect our daily lives, but it is incredibly common for children to suffer from anxiety as well. For children, anxiety can look like a tantrum, wanting attention, or defiance. Knowing what anxiety is and how it can affect your child will allow you to help your child address and overcome what is making them anxious.

What Is Anxiety?

Anxiety is a natural response when you feel stress. If can cause you to feel afraid of certain situations, people, or things. Feeling anxious about things is a normal and healthy part of development. All children will feel anxious from time to time. It is a normal phase that will come and go as your child grows.

Children may feel anxious when they have seen a scary movie, had a doctor's appointment, are starting their first day of school, or when they are meeting new people. With reassurance and support, most children are able to easily move past their scary feelings and go about their day. Anxiety is often harmless for children to experience.

When a child begins to avoid certain places, people, or things because of their anxiety is when it becomes a problem that needs to be addressed.

Even with reassurance and support from their parents, their anxiety can feel overwhelming and frightening to the point where they are unable to confront what is causing them these extreme feelings.

Children can just as easily develop an anxiety disorder as teens and adults can. If left untreated, a child's anxiety disorder can affect many areas of their life such as school, friendships, and participating in fun activities. It can also impact their sleep, diet, mood and behavior. Children who suffer from anxiety disorders are more likely to develop depression.

How to Recognize Anxiety in Children

It can be a challenge to detect anxiety in young children. Children often do not know how to properly express their concerns or may not have the skills yet to even recognize that they are feeling anxious. Their lack of understanding of their emotions may cause them to act out in inappropriate ways or cause them to feel embarrassed about being scared or frightened all the time. Many children try to hide what they are really feeling simply because they don't understand it themselves.

Anxiety can present itself in a number of ways and these signs can often be confused with other conditions like ADHD. Your child may be more restless, hyper, emotional, or withdrawn. Some common anxiety disorders your child may be suffering from include:

1. **Generalized Anxiety Disorder**

Generalized anxiety disorder (GAD) occurs when your child excessively worries every day. There is not one specific thing that they become worried about, instead, they worry about a number of things. Some of these things are typical for children such as worrying about taking a test or making friends. But, a child with GAD will worry about these things to an extreme and the worry will be more than just how well they do on a test or if someone will sit next to them during circle time.

Children with GAD worry more deeply, such as if they will disappoint their parents, how smart they appear to others, and if their parents will still love them after making a mistake. These children will also worry about much bigger issues such as if a tornado will occur when it begins to rain or about future events that will occur when they are adults.

When a child is suffering from GAD they struggle to focus and stay on task. They will often seem unhappy and be unable to enjoy fun activities. This constant worry can cause them to become physically sick and interrupt their sleep. Even when reassured that what they are worrying about should not be a concern, the child is unable to stay focused or feel safe.

2. Separation Anxiety Disorder

Most children suffer from a mild form of separation anxiety, especially when they are first left with a babysitter or starting school. After a short period of time, however, many kids will forget that they are away from their parents and will be able to participate in activities and move on in the day. Many children are able to feel safe and secure in their new settings quickly. Children who are unable to feel safe and secure unless their parents are in sight or next to them develop separation anxiety disorder (SAD).

Children with SAD become incredibly anxious when they are away from their parents and this anxiousness doesn't go away over time or as they grow older. It may be difficult for a child with SAD to even be in their own home unless their parent or caregiver is in the same room as them. A child who suffers from SAD may try to avoid situations where they know their parents will not be around. They can also become ill from the anxiety they feel from being away from the parent.

3. Social Anxiety

Social phobia or social anxiety disorder occurs when a child becomes seriously afraid of being around or talking when others are around them. Children suffering from this type of anxiety tend to fear what others may think of them. They are in a constant state of fear of doing something wrong or making a mistake. This causes the child to avoid participating in group activities, answering questions at school, or appearing to be shy when around other people. Many parents mistake their child's social anxiety with them just being shy, and this can cause the child to normalize their behavior which results in it continuing and becoming more extreme. When a child with social anxiety is forced to try to talk in front of others or perform a task, such as being called on in class to answer a question or having attention put on them for being shy, they begin to panic.

Extreme cases of social anxiety can result in selective mutism. In these cases, your child may be so afraid to talk to others they simply do not talk.

With selective mutism your child may refuse to talk in school, with their friends, or when out in the community.

4. Phobias

Children can develop specific phobias at a very young age. It is not uncommon for children to be afraid of the dark, loud noises, or certain animals. In many of these instances, an adult can help them feel safe and secure in these situations and the child can calm themselves down and face what they fear. Phobias that become more intense or extreme and last much longer can cause extreme feelings of dread in a child. Children who have specific phobias will do whatever they can think of to avoid confronting what is causing them anxiety. If a child thinks they may confront what they fear they will avoid going to places.

Why Your Child Is Anxious

A child will begin to feel anxious when their body senses any form of danger. Some of the first indication a child may experience when they become anxious is an increase in their heart rate, feeling shaky or jittery, having a hard time catching their breath, or feeling clammy or sweaty. Anxiety can develop because of a number of factors such as:

- Genetics
- Brain chemistry
- Life experiences

- Learned behaviors

One or all of these factors may be causing your child to suffer from anxiety. You can learn to spot specific signs of anxiety at home and in school.

Behaviors at home

Parents may notice some signs of anxiety more easily than others at home.

- Your child may be sleeping less, waking frequently throughout the night or having night terrors or nightmares.
- Their eating habits might change suddenly. Children who are anxious may eat less.
- Mood changes are also common. Your children may become more irritable have an uncontrollable emotional outburst or may get angry in general each day. Your child may cry more or become upset much easier than they used to.
- Children with anxiety may use the restroom more often.
- Your child may have more negative thoughts or constantly be worrying.
- If your child seems to cling to your more often or follow you around wherever you go more than usual, they may be feeling anxious. Children may have a more difficult time going to school, attending birthday parties, or not having a parent or caregiver in sight at all times.
- Anxiety may present itself in the form of feeling physically ill. Your child may complain of stomach aches or headaches.

- Anxious children will often ask "what if" questions that can sound morbid or random.

- Children suffering from anxiety might have fears or worry about future events.

- They can become overly emotional or frustrated when they make a simple mistake.

Behaviors at school

If you are concerned about your child's anxiety, you can ask their teachers if they have noticed any issues. Your child's teacher may be able notice if they possibly have a learning disability that is contributing to the anxiety. Additionally, teachers will be able to inform you if your child may be exhibit any of the following concerns.

- Children may be unable to concentrate or focus as they used to. They may become distracted easily. They will often have a hard time completing seatwork.

- Children with anxiety are often more fidgety. They may appear to be tense or nervous.

- They may not like to participate in group activities like circle time or recess.

- Children may immediately say they cannot do something when given work or ask to complete a task.

- Children with anxiety can have frequent meltdowns.

- They might have difficulty transitioning from one activity to the next.

How to React to an Anxious Child

A child suffering from anxiety can be a challenge. Parents may be trying their best to keep their child calm but can become quickly frustrated by their child's behaviors. Helping your anxious child will also require additional focus on yourself as their parents. It can be exhausting for parents to constantly be supporting and working with their child to help overcome their anxiety and this can lead parents to feel isolated and alone in the daily struggles they are having with their child. Just as you want to do everything to help your child, you also need to give yourself the same love and consideration. Join support groups and talk about any unwanted feelings with a therapist or trusted friend or loved one. The more you feel supported, the better you will be able to help your child.

Be encouraging when your child attempts to face their fears. You do not want to force your child to confront what they are afraid of, as these can be a traumatic experience for the child. Instead, allow your child to take small steps in confronting their fears and let them know you notice their efforts. You can help your child become more comfortable with their anxiety by slowly exposing them to what they are afraid of. This can be done by showing them pictures of what they are afraid of, talking to them about situations that make them anxious, or role-playing situations where they feel anxious.

Talk regularly with your child about how they are feeling. You should reassure your child that you are there to support them and help them feel safe. The more you talk with your child about how they are feeling the more your child will be able to understand what is causing their fear and how they can better cope with these fears.

Exercises

Identify anxiety

Have your child answer and complete the sentences below. You can provide them with examples as listed so they can better understand how they can identify their own emotions in specific situations and the cues their body gives. Then brainstorm activities your child can do to help them feel better when they are experiencing these emotions.

I feel anxious when…

- I have to talk in class
- I met someone new
- I see a big dog
- My parents take me to school
- I have to eat in front of other people
- I am alone

When I am anxious…

- My heart beats faster
- I begin to sweat

- My stomach gets upset or feels like there are butterflies flying around
- I feel shaky
- My head, ears, or body begin to feel hot.
- My palms begin to sweat or feel wet.

When I feel anxious I can...

- Take a deep breath
- Talk to someone about what is bothering me.
- Draw a picture.
- Listen to music.

I FEEL ANXIOUS WHEN:

_____

_____

_____

WHEN I FEEL ANXIOUS MY BODY:

_____

_____

_____

WHEN I FEEL ANXIOUS I CAN:

_____

_____

_____

For parents

Create an anxiety log. This will help you recognize patterns in your child's behavior. You can ask teachers to give you insight and track your child's behavior at school so you can work as a team to better assist your child.

Sample anxiety log

Date:
Time of day:
What was happening before you noticed your child became anxious?
What were the physical, emotional, or behavioral signs you noticed?
Did anything help calm your child down?
How long did it take for your child to calm down?
How intense was your child's anxiety (rate from 1-10)?

How stressed did your child's anxiety makes you feel (rate from 1-10)?

Chapter 4: Depression

Feeling sad or in a down mood is normal. It is ok to be disappointed and feel blue from time to time, even for children. Sadness is a core emotion that can be triggered by a number of outside or internal factors. A child may feel sad when they don't get their favorite snack, when a crayon breaks, or when more traumatic life occurrences happens. But, just as with adults or teens, sadness can transition into a more concerning condition if it progresses for long periods of time.

What Is Depression?

Depression is considered a mood disorder that occurs when there are long periods (weeks, months, or even years) of feeling a deep sadness. Children who suffer from this type of mood disorder will be riddled with negative thoughts about themselves, others, or the world around them. They can become overly critical, complain excessively, and only focus on problems instead of trying to find solutions.

Depression is a serious condition that can affect concentration, sleep, appetite, and a child's energy levels. It will also make it more challenging for the child to participate in activities and develop proper social skills. Depression can cause a child to withdraw from their friends and family. Children who are depressed will struggle to complete tasks, will give up when faced with even the smallest of challenges and this only feeds into the disorder.

When a child is depressed their self-esteem can become greatly affected. They will often feel incapable of doing things, feel worthless, and will exaggerate everyday problems. Depression knows no age limits. Many parents think their young child could not possibly be suffering from depression because it is viewed as being an adult disorder. But, depression can affect children in the same way it affects adults but to a higher degree.

Children lack a number of coping skills and the emotional intelligence many adults have developed to navigate through depressive states. This leads to children having a more difficult time expressing what they are feeling appropriately Children will often react with anger or frustration, may pretend to be ill, or may not even be aware of the feelings they are feeling. As a parent, knowing how to spot signs of depression in your young child can help you help them in a more effective way.

How to Recognize Depression in Children

Depression is often overlooked in children for a number of reasons. Often, parents do not recognize the warning signs simply because they think their child is too young to become depressed. Any event that occurs, even if it may not seem like it could traumatize your child, may have a long-lasting impression on them. They may have witnessed someone getting hurt, and although the individual may be perfectly fine, a young child will often misinterpret these events and can become fearful of it happening to their parents or caregivers. This can cause the child to focus on some negative possibility that consumes them causing them to have intense, prolonged periods of sadness.

That said, depression will always have symptoms that you as the parent or caregiver can be aware of.

Why your child is depressed

There are a number of factors that can contribute to childhood depression. Medical conditions such as diabetes or epilepsy, life events, troubles at home, or a family history of depression can cause a child to be more prone to developing depression in their young lives. If the child has suffered from a form of abuse, whether physical or verbal, they are more likely to become depressed. There are symptoms that you can keep a watch for that may give you an indication that your child is suffering from more than just a case of the blues.

Behaviors at home

- Your child may appear to be more on edge or irritable.
- Persistent feelings of being sad or hopeless.
- They may become withdrawn and spend more time alone.
- They are overly sensitive to criticism.
- Change in their sleep, either sleep more often than usual or not enough.

- Change in appetite.
- Having increased temper tantrums.
- They may appear to be more fatigued or have lower energy they usual.
- They may complain of stomach aches or headaches frequently.
- Your child may make comments about feeling worthless or feeling guilty over things that are out of their control.
- They may become more focused on death, or even talk about not wanting to be around anymore.

Behaviors at school

- The child may appear to be lethargic.
- They are unable to focus or concentrate on classwork.
- They withdraw from friends and choose not to participate in group activities.
- They are no longer interested in activities they once enjoyed doing.
- They are quick to anger.
- They feel defeated or are unwilling to try new things.

A child may not show any signs of depression in one setting but will show increased signs in another. For example, a child may appear to be happy and fine at home but at school they may be more anxious and withdrawn. Children can cycle through symptoms where there may be times when they are more temperamental as opposed to withdrawn and vice versa. Though it is unlikely that really young children will attempt physical harm it can occur because they act on impulse. If your child is acting out violently

41

where they pose a threat to themselves or to others around them professional help is necessary.

Depression can be overcome. The child needs to learn to gain control and recognize what is causing them the intense feelings. Parents can show support and love to their child while working with them to develop skills that will improve their lives significantly and these skills will be valuable as they grow older.

How to React to a Depressed Child

If you notice your child may have signs of depression, your first reaction should be to get them the help they need. Getting a diagnosis for depression can be challenging as many of the depression disorders require the child to have symptoms that persist for a year or more. But, even without an official diagnosis, there are ways you can help your child open up about what they are feeling.

Many young children may not understand that they are depressed and therefore resist help or deny that they are feeling so down. Talking with your child is one of the best things you can do to help them. The key to getting your child to open up about what they are feeling is to be present and listen to them when they are talking. You want to show your child that you are there for them to provide them support and love.

Schedule in extra time to connect with your child. Many are unaware of how distracted they are when it comes to spending time with their children. There may be constant interruptions from work or other family members when you are with your child. But dedicating a short amount of time to just play and be with your child, without interruptions, can help them feel less alone and more cared for. Schedule activities that your child likes to do and make time to just relax, laugh, and do something together.

Helping your depressed child will take patience and understanding. Children may act out more aggressively when they are depressed. They may be moodier or more emotional, which can cause parents to become easily frustrated. While it may seem as though your child is purposely being disrespectful or uncooperative, understand that reacting with kindness and love is more effective than reacting with anger and authority. Keep in mind how challenging it is for many adults to navigate this disorder and give yourself and your child some credit as both of you work together to overcome it.

Another key factor to consider is your child's lifestyle. A child that is not getting enough sleep, exercise, or nutritious foods is more likely to suffer from depression. These key factors can also make depression symptoms worse. Be sure your child is eating healthy meals, doing some form of physical activity and getting enough sleep each day. By ensuring these three factors are being met each day, you may notice a significant change in their mood.

CBT is an effective way that many children can learn to overcome their depression and learn skills that will help them avoid falling into this state in the future. Bringing in a specialist to help you and your child is an effective way both of you can learn how to respond to these overwhelming emotions. Not only will CBT work with the child to address the root cause of the depression, but parents will also learn useful tools that they can use to assist their child when they are faced with the challenging situations that can lead to depression.

Exercise

Identifying sadness

With your child, discuss and complete the sentences below. You can provide them with examples as listed so they can better understand how they can identify their own emotions in specific situations and the cues their body gives. Then brainstorm activities your child can do to help them feel better when they are experiencing these emotions.

I feel sad when...

- No one sits with me at lunch.
- My friends do not say "Hi" to me.
- I see someone else get hurt.
- I do something wrong or bad.
- I get in trouble or yelled at.

When I'm sad my body feels...

- Tired
- Weak
- Achy

When I'm sad I can ...

- Ask for a hug
- Talk to someone
- Do something fun
- Laugh
- Tell a joke
- Go for a walk
- Listen to music

I FEEL SAD WHEN:

_____

_____

_____

WHEN I FEEL SAD MY BODY:

_____

_____

_____

WHEN I FEEL SAD I CAN:

_____

_____

_____

Chapter 5: Stress

it can be difficult to understand how a child can suffer from stress. They are supposed to be enjoying their young lives and unaware of the external demands that their parents are stressing over. Children can be highly aware of the stress others are feeling and this can cause them to feel anxious and overwhelmed. Children can also suffer from stress because they are still learning how to properly organize themselves.

What Is Stress?

Stress occurs when we feel overwhelmed or out of control. Our thoughts play a major role in the stress we experience because it is our minds that begin to cause feelings of anxiety and of being overwhelmed. The thoughts we play over in our heads that revolve around certain situations can cause us to feel as though we have no control over what is happening. Stress is a common occurrence when we begin to focus too much on the person we should be as opposed to what we are actually capable of.

For children. this can arise when they feel they have disappointed their parents, when they struggle to understand or learn new things as quickly as others, or when their parents are unable to give them the attention they have been used to. As children grow older they begin to learn to do things for themselves, this is a normal part of healthy development. Some children, however, find these extra responsibilities to be overwhelming when they are applied all at once.

A child may be able to do a great deal for themselves. If the task is broken up and there is plenty of downtime in between one task and another. When these tasks come at them one after another they can quickly lose sight of their capabilities and become overwhelmed by what is expected of them. Parents may not understand why the task is so complex for their child. You may know your child is capable of brushing their teeth, getting dressed and putting on their shoes by themselves. But when you give them all these tasks to do in a set order your child freaks out and all of the sudden doesn't know what to do as though they have never completed the task before on their own.

How to Recognize Stress in Children

Young children have a more difficult time identifying stress and understanding the toll it is taking on their emotions, thoughts, and behaviors. Children who are attending school can feel more stressed as they are learning more challenging things, are trying to make and keep friends, and doing their best to please their teachers and parents. All these elements can lead to a child feeling overwhelmed and unable to control themselves. Children typically act out when they do not know what to do when they are feeling stress as they often have no way of knowing what is causing them to feel the way they feel or how to verbalize what they are feeling.

Why your child is stressed

It is not uncommon for children to suffer from stress. Children who are just beginning school or entering daycare can suffer from separation anxiety which makes them feel overwhelmed and fearful. Additionally, parents who talk about how stressed they are or worried they are about things in their life like finances or health concerns may have a child that takes on these worries themselves. When your child begins discussing or voicing concerns about your job, how bills will be paid, or about a relative or their own health they have most likely overheard these concerns being voiced by the parent. While it is considerate of them to be concerned, what often occurs is that they become stressed about these matters simply because their parents are unknowingly passing these concerns onto them.

Sudden changes in their routine can cause stress. Children thrive on structure. They like to know what to expect and are able to adapt fairly well when they understand how their day is going to run. When this routine is disrupted, children can be overly stressed as they no longer know what to expect. They are not able to go with the flow because they have become used to doing things a certain way for so long. The break in their regular routine can throw off their whole thought process off.

Stress, just as with other concerning mental issues, can be challenging to detect in younger children. They may exhibit mood swings and tantrums that are typical for children. When these short-term behaviors begin to occur more frequently and sporadically this can be a red flag that your child is overly stressed.

Behaviors at home

- Your child may act out more than they typically would.
- They may begin to wet the bed more frequently or unexpectedly.
- They may complain of frequent headaches.
- Your child may have more frequent mood swings.
- Their sleep patterns may change.
- They may begin to suck their thumb or begin other comforting habits such as hair twirling or picking at their nails.
- Your child may overreact to minor mistakes.
- They may become clingier to their parents or caregiver.

Behaviors at school

- A stressed child will be unable to concentrate in the classroom.
- They may become defiant and act out randomly when asked to complete a task or follow expected rules.
- They might not complete classwork or turning in homework.
- The child may withdraw from friends or prefer to spend time by themselves.
- They may struggle to participate in group activities.
- Their academic performance may decrease significantly.

How to React to a Stressed Child

If you notice your child may be suffering from stress, the first thing you want to consider and be more mindful of is what and how you talk about the things that are causing you stress. As mentioned, children will quickly pick up on their parents' stress and concerns. Next, you want to ensure that your child is getting enough sleep and eating a healthy diet. When your child is well-rested they are less likely to be irritable and will be able to focus better. When they eat healthy, they will be less likely to feel sluggish or lethargic.

Scheduling in plenty of exercise is also ideal. Physical activity is one of the best ways to reduce stress for both the parent and the child. It also provides an opportunity to spend quality time with your child. This doesn't have to be going for a run or doing sit-ups, simply doing something that your child enjoys doing like dancing around the living room or racing cars bath and forth in a room can be enough. Not only do these play activities get them moving it shows that you are interested in what they want to do.

Talking with your child about what they are feeling can help you understand their behaviors and identify the thoughts that contribute to their stress. When you talk with your child, listen closely to what they are saying and work with your child to come up with some solutions for how they can better manage and react to the thoughts and feelings they are struggling with.

Not all stress is bad. Minor stress helps a child develop properly but they need to learn how to handle the stress in appropriate ways. As a parent, you can model effective ways to manage stress and allow your child to join in when you practice stress-reducing activities. Below you will find a few examples of how to help your child identify what is causing the stress and activities you can do together to reduce stress.

Exercises

Identifying stress

Have your child consider the prompts below. You can provide them with the examples so they can better understand how they can identify their own emotions in specific situations and pick up on the cues their body gives. Then brainstorm activities your child can do to help them feel better when they are experiencing these emotions.

I feel stressed when…

- There is too much noise.
- My parents fight.
- I forget something for school.
- I don't know the answer to something.
- I am asked to do too many things.
- I can't remember what I am supposed to be doing.
- I can't find anything I need.

When I feel stressed by body feels…

- Shaky
- My head hurts
- My body feels tired
- My heart feels like it is racing

When I am stressed I can…

- Ask for help
- Take a deep breath and count to five
- Read a book
- Listen to calming music
- Go for a walk
- Color

I FEEL STRESSED WHEN:

_____

_____

_____

WHEN I FEEL STRESSED MY BODY:

_____

_____

_____

WHEN I FEEL STRESSED I CAN:

_____

_____

_____

Chapter 6: Anger

An angry child can be a serious concern. Their frustration can cause them to act out in harmful and unsafe manners. Children who express their anger in unhealthy ways such as hitting, throwing, harming themselves, or causing harm to others need help in learning suitable ways to express what they are feeling and how to cope with these feelings. Parents who have experienced these extreme, out of control, moments with their child know how scary these moments can be. Taking the time to teach your child and addressing the issues early on will allow them to develop the necessary skills to gain control over themselves and their emotions.

What Is Anger?

Anger is a common emotion we all feel. It can cause us to react immediately to what we feel is unfair, frightening, or stressful. This emotion can come on quickly and in the moment we can temporarily lose control over our impulses.

Anger is especially difficult for a child to manage. They often react intensely to feeling frustrated and this can lead to hitting, biting, throwing objects, screaming and other over-the-top behaviors. Once the feeling has run its course, the child is able to immediately calm down and will be remorseful for the way they acted. What needs to be understood is your child's behavior may be the only way they know how to communicate to you what they are feeling.

Throwing, hitting, screaming, and other dangerous reactions to anger is common for a child that does not know how to express themselves in any other manner. Anger can cause your child to become quickly overwhelmed. They may not yet have the skills necessary to solve the problem they are facing, use their words instead of their body, or control the impulses and intensity when they feel angry.

Many immediately think of this type of behavior as the child simply acting out negatively to get attention or to get what they want. While young children may exhibit this type of behavior to get their needs met it is more likely that they are unable to tell you what they need or want in a more appropriate manner. How you as the parent react to these bouts of frustration from your child can either strengthen the behaviors or allow them to learn more effective ways to handle this extreme emotion.

How to Recognize Anger in Children

Children who suffer from ADHD, anxiety, learning disabilities, sensory processing issues, or autism will have frequent violent outbursts. Each of these diagnoses makes it more challenging for a child to process their emotions and express properly what is troubling them. Not all children have an underlying condition that causes their anger. Many children simply lack the skills or are unable to understand what they are feeling to respond to the situation in a way that is favorable.

Why your child is angry

Children express their anger in uncontrollable ways from lashing out to throwing things or speaking unkindly. When a child is acting out aggressively, they are letting you know they are in a state of distress. They often lack vital skills such as being able to communicate properly, control their impulses or using coping mechanisms or problem-solving abilities. While tantrums are normal for younger children, when they continue past the age of seven and become more intense, this is a red flag that your child is struggling to control their frustrations.

Behaviors at home

- Your child may have extreme, aggressive outbursts regularly.
- Your child may exhibit dangerous behavior when they are angry and may harm themselves or others around them.
- They may experience frequent and long-lasting tantrums.
- The child's behavior may be causing additional stress or strain on the family members.
- Your child may be remorseful and begin to feel negatively about him/herself because they are unable to control their anger.

Behaviors at school

- Teachers may view an aggressive child as out of control.

- The child will struggle to get along with others.
- Classmates may exclude an aggressive child.

How to React to an Angry Child

The best thing you can do when your child is angry is to stay calm. It can be challenging to remain composed and not let your child's behavior affect how you react to their outburst. Keep in mind your kid's behavior may be the only way they know how to communicate their frustration and this often is done in unhealthy and unsafe ways. When you remain calm you are modeling how they can remain calm when they become frustrated. When you respond aggressively to your child's behavior may only reinforce the behavior or give your child the impression that you do not care or are not listening to what they need. They may not be telling you directly what they need but yelling back at your child will not help them solve their problem.

Your child's behavior can be extremely frustrating, especially when they are acting out because they are not getting what they want. It is important that you stay firm in your choices. Caving in and giving your child what they want just to get them to stop the inappropriate behavior only teaches them that this type of behavior will eventually get them what they want. It can be tempting to just give them what they want to make them stop but this will cause the behavior to worsen and the behavior will continue for years.

Give praise to your child when they are able to calm themselves done. You want to encourage your child to react appropriately when they are feeling angry and this will talk a great deal of praise to let them know what exactly they are doing correctly. When your child attempts to express their feelings verbally, tell them they are doing a great job at remaining calm and trying to communicate with you about what is upsetting them. If your child works with you to find a compromise to what has angered them, praise them again. Every effort your child makes to respond to their anger in a mature manner, give them praise for their efforts.

What about time outs?

Time outs can be an effective way to help your child better control and understand there are consequences for their behavior. If your child is under eight years of age, time outs can be a way for them to calm down and then discuss what happened. If your child is over the age of eight, then time outs may not be effective. In these cases, some parents have success with rewards or point system when the child exhibits appropriate behaviors.

Keep in mind, reward systems do not always help a child understand their behavior. When setting up a reward system you want to know what types of behavior you will reward. Some things you can reward include:

- Your child speaks to you with a calm voice even though they are frustrated.
- They take a deep breath when they are getting angry or use another calm technique you have discussed.

- They ask you for help when they are trying to solve a problem.

There are many positive behaviors you can reward but you want to ensure that your child is developing the skills they need to manage their anger. If they are not making efforts to remain in control of themselves aside from seeking out a prize, then a reward system may not be the best option.

Additional suggestions

Notice what triggers your child's anger. Many times situations, activities, settings, or even the clothes they are wearing can be a trigger for meltdowns. When you can identify triggers you will be able to assist your child better in preparing themselves for how to handle what is coming up. So, things you can do to help your child work through their triggers:

1. Establish a routine.

You have probably already heard how much children thrive when there is structure in their day and there is a lot of truth in this. When you establish a routine with your child, they already know what to expect. There is less of a chance that they will become frustrated when it is time to do homework or get ready for bed. Create a routine helps your child feel more confident and safe.

When changes to your schedule do occur, as they will often, be sure that you talk about the upcoming changes in advance with your child. Some kids can easily adjust when they are told something different is going on in their day. Other children may need to be reminded a few days in advance.

If you know there will be a change in your child's typical routine, it is best to let your child know ahead of time so they can be prepared.

2. Use timers/give time-based warnings.

If your child gets easily frustrated when it is time to move on to the next activity in the day, giving verbal warnings or setting timers can be a huge help. You want to ensure your child understands that the activity they are currently preoccupied with will need to end soon and another activity will be taking place. When you begin to implement warnings and timers you might need to give a number of them a half-hour prior to the transition. This may seem nagging your child but it helps them prepare for what is coming.

When you use verbal warnings or timers you need to have your child's attention so that you know they understand what will be expected of them. If your child is busy playing with cars or dolls as you are telling them they have 10 minutes left before they have to put the toys away you might get an "Ok," but your child may not have processed what you have said at all. Get down to your child's level and explain to them in simple terms that playtime will be over soon, let them know that you will give them a warning when they have "X" amount of time left, and when the timer goes off it is time to move on to the next activity.

3. Have them repeat what is expected of them.

Many children get distracted easily and do a fantastic job of tuning out what parents and caregivers say to them. This quickly leads to frustration and meltdowns when a child thinks it is unfair that you get to make all the choices. If you have a constant power struggle with your child that triggers an angry outburst it can simply be because your child is not actually processing what you are saying to them and therefore has no idea what is expected of them.

When you are giving warnings, going over consequences, or giving them directions to do something you want to get down to their level and have them repeat back what you have said. Depending on their age you will need to simplify what you are saying or the steps you are giving so they can easily remember what you just said. Do not let them continue with an activity they are currently engaged in if they do not repeat back what you have said. There will be a great deal of resistance when you use these techniques with your child for a number of reasons. You may need to repeat yourself a few times before what you said actually sticks in your child's brain, but staying calm and patient will help your child remain calm and patient.

4. **Use pictures or lists.**

Younger children may need to have visuals to help them stay on track and to remind them how to stay calm when they are feeling frustrated. You can hang pictures of calming techniques or of what is on the daily schedule so your child knows where to look to know what to do when they are upset and to also know what is coming up next in the day.

Older children can help you create a task list or daily schedule of how the day will unfold. You can create trackers that help them know everything they need to get done in terms of chores, homework, or activities.

Visuals are great in helping children learn how to calm down since they are able to better recall a picture they see over words that are said to them.

Exercises

Identifying anger

Have your child answer and complete the sentence below. You can provide them with the examples as listed so they can better understand how they can identify their own emotions in specific situations and better understand the cues their body gives. Then brainstorm activities your child can do to help them feel better when they are experiencing these emotions.

I feel angry when...

- I get told no.
- Someone else is playing with a toy I want.
- I don't get what I want.
- I make a mistake.
- Someone does not do what I want them too.
- I can't find what I am looking for.
- I hear loud noises.
- My socks aren't on right.

When I feel angry my body:

- Feels hot

- Feels tense
- My stomach hurts
- My head begins to pound
- My heart beats harder
- It is harder to breath

When I am angry I can…

- Take a deep breath
- Walk away from the situation until I am calm
- Color
- Do jumping jacks
- Draw a picture of what made me angry
- Ask for help
- Go somewhere quiet

I FEEL ANGRY WHEN:

_____

_____

_____

WHEN I FEEL ANGRY MY BODY:

_____

_____

_____

WHEN I FEEL ANGRY I CAN:

_____

_____

Drawing

Have your child draw a picture of what their anger looks like. This does not and should not be a picture of themselves, instead, it should be a character that your child creates.

Once your child has created their picture have them give their anger a name. You can now use this drawing your child made to help them identify when their anger is coming out. You can use the name your child gave to the drawing to name their own anger. This helps your child distinguish between their own emotions and responses and those that are occurring because of their anger.

Chapter 7: Trauma

It is not uncommon for children to be exposed to traumatic events. Any form of violence both severe and small can cause a child to feel traumatized. Witnessing a neighbor being taken to the hospital can be traumatic. Seeing a family member become extremely upset or violent can be traumatic for a child. You never want to think of your child as being exposed to traumatic events but it is most likely they already have been. Though it is not unhealthy for a child to experience mild forms of trauma, any type of exposure can lead to serious problems for the child. By understanding what trauma may look and feel like your child you may be able to identify what is causing some of the behavior or emotional issues your child is struggling with.

What Is Trauma?

Trauma occurs when something life-threatening occurs to a person. It can also be the result of physical or personal security being threatened. For a child, this can be anything that causes them to become incredibly fearful or frightened. Children who suffer from trauma feel helpless and unsafe. Children can react strongly to certain situations that can cause them to feel traumatized even if there was no real threat to their life or the life of a loved one.

Traumatic events can include those involving:

- Abuse, either witnessing someone close to them being abused or being abused themselves.
- Domestic violence
- Violence in the community
- Violence in school
- Car accidents
- Illness
- Natural disasters

For a child, experiencing trauma can be incredibly frightening. In many situations, the child is able to be comforted and made to feel safe in a short amount of time. Other children may suffer from a traumatic event that many parents are completely unaware of. Sudden behavioral changes are a clear indication that your child may be suffering from trauma. You may be completely unaware of what could have caused your child to feel traumatized and only by deliberately listening to what your child says and their explanation will you be able to uncover what the true cause is.

How to Recognize Trauma in Children

Many parents dismiss certain events as harmless to their child. But, these events can cause a child to form unrealistic views of the world around them. For example, a child may have witnessed a neighbor being taken away in an ambulance just before they are about to go to school. After school, the child may see this neighbor and know that they are completely fine and nothing is wrong with them. All day at school, however, the child may not only be thinking about the neighbor but may also begin to worry about their parents. They may develop an intense fear that something bad has happened to them while they were at school. Even after the child sees the neighbor is fine, they still may not be able to stop worrying that something may happen to their parents. This simple event can cause the child to be traumatized and they may begin to try to miss out on going to school in order to be sure that nothing has happened to their parents.

As a parent, you may not have even remembered the incident with the neighbor. Only when talking to your child will this detail be revealed. Then you can begin to help your child feel safer and reassure them that them going to school does not mean that their parents are in danger.

Understand the trauma your child is suffering from

Trauma can occur at any age. The younger the child is, the more difficult it is for them to communicate what is causing them to feel so frightened and unsafe. Childhood trauma will typically fall into three categories; acute, chronic, or complex. Understanding the type of trauma your child may be suffering from can help you and your child work through the

1. Acute trauma

Acute trauma occurs after just a single event. This can be witnessing a violent act in the community, car accidents, or the sudden loss of a loved one to name a few. After an acute traumatic event, the child will experience some form of distress that is often short-term. The distress they feel tends to be reflected in their behavior as a way to cope with what they are feeling. With support from loved ones, children who suffer from acute trauma are able to transition easily back into the "normal" behaviors prior to the event.

2. Chronic trauma

This type of trauma is the result of experiencing repeated traumatic events. Children who are exposed to domestic violence or who are or have been abused will develop chronic trauma. Most children do their best to simply ignore or avoid the repeated events, hoping they can just address the issue later or that it will go away. The longer the child tries to ignore this event, the more their negative behaviors will increase and the more likely that they will develop physical manifestations such as chronic headaches or stomach pains.

3. Complex trauma

Complex trauma is the result of continuous exposure to traumatic events. These events are invasive and/or interpersonal such as abuse or neglect. Complex trauma is similar to chronic trauma as it is a repeated event but, complex trauma tends to occur to the child and not just be witnessed by the child. Many times complex trauma is brought on by someone who is supposed to be a trusted caregiver to the child. As a result, the child is unable to form proper attachments with adults or peers. The child will suffer from long term distress making is especially challenging for the child to feel safe and cared for. Other long-term effects can lower the child's self-esteem, and they develop a negative self-image.

Behaviors at home

- Intense emotional outbursts
- Your child may not leave your side or will become anxious if you are out of sight.
- Frequent nightmares
- Trouble falling asleep
- Change in appetite
- Complaints of body aches or pains that have no known cause.
- Your child may appear to be depressed.
- Your child may begin to suck their thumb.
- Becomes fearful of the future
- Children who suffer from trauma may begin to wet the bed.

Behaviors at school

- Children will often show signs of separation anxiety.
- The child will begin to struggle with completing tasks that were never a challenge before.
- The child will struggle to interact with peers.
- Children will have sudden behavioral changes often time disruptive behaviors.
- A child suffering from trauma may not be able to relate to their peers.
- The student may have more difficulty completing schoolwork.
- They may be unable to concentrate.

How to Behave When a Child Has Suffered a Trauma

Your child is feeling a loss of security and be struggling with upsetting thoughts and unpleasant emotions. They need your reassurance that they are safe and this can take constant reminding. Be understanding of their feelings and fears. You don't want to force your child to talk about what occurred unless they are ready and willing to. When they are ready to talk and listen to them and take their concerns seriously.

Limit their exposure to news reports. While you don't want to ignore what happened, you don't want them to have to relive the trauma by hearing news coverage on it. If you do allow your child to watch the news watch with them and talk about what is being reported on.

Reassure your child that it is OK to feel what they are feeling. Do not discredit their emotions or telling them not to feel a certain way. This can lead to your child bottling up big emotions instead of addressing them and working through them. Let your child know how you are feeling too. You may not be feeling the same way but this can let your child learn that everyone reacts differently to certain events. It also helps them recognize that everyone struggles with big emotions, even adults. This can help them feel less alone, embarrassed, or ashamed by what they are feeling.

Schedule in extra one-on-one time with your child. If a traumatic event occurred in your community, then show them that they are still safe and able to have fun doing the things they used to love doing. Show them lots of support and help them talk about their feelings in a way that lets them feel secure and comforted. When a child has suffered through a traumatic event it is important that you remind them they can still have fun. Allow them plenty of time to simply play.

It is important that you maintain regular structure when a traumatic event occurs. Going about your day as you typically would help your child feel more secure. If you are unable to stick to the exact routine you once had, reassure your child that things will return to the way they once were. Do not push your child to do more or give them new responsibilities or chores. Working through trauma can be intense for a child and giving them more to manage can cause extreme behavioral challenges.

Exercises

Identifying worry

Have your child answer and complete the sentences below. You can provide them with the listed examples, so they can better understand how they can identify their own emotions in specific situations and recognize the cues their body gives. Then brainstorm activities your child can do to help them feel better when they are experiencing these emotions.

I feel worried when…

- I am not near my parents.
- I am in an unfamiliar place.
- There are a lot of people near me.

- I have to go to school.
- We drive in the car.
- I hear loud noises.
- I smell smoke.

When I am worried my body feels...

- Shaky
- My head hurts
- My heart begins to be faster
- My palms feel sweaty or cold and clammy
- I may feel weak and tired

When I am worried I can…

- Talk to someone about how I am feeling
- Take a deep breath.
- Ask myself if what I am thinking is true?
- Tell myself that I am safe.

I FEEL WORRIED WHEN:

_____

_____

_____

WHEN I FEEL WORRIED MY BODY:

_____

_____

_____

WHEN I FEEL WORRIED I CAN:

_____

_____

_____

Chapter 8: Attention Deficit Hyperactivity Disorder (ADHD)

Attention deficit hyperactivity disorder (ADHD) is a condition that can impact a child for the rest of their lives. Getting the proper diagnosis and understanding any additional conditions that can be confused and coincide with ADHD is vital for the child to be successful. This condition is more than just behavioral issues, despite what most understand of it. ADHD can negatively impact many areas of a child's life and this in turn will impact their teenage and adult lives.

What Is ADHD?

ADHD makes it more difficult for a child to focus, sit still, and display self-control. This condition is a result of developmental delays in the brain as well as confusion in brain activity. A child with ADHD will struggle at home, in school, and making friends.

Children with ADHD struggle with following directions, even if they are only given instructions with two or three steps. They are unable to stay on task and need constant redirection or reminding. They often miss important details when given a task to complete. Many children can begin a task but never complete it often leading them to be viewed as lazy, forgetful, or defiant.

Hyperactivity is a common symptom of ADHD but a child may display this symptom in varying ways. Some children may literally bounce around the room, run back and forth, or appear to be running on a motor. Others may simply fidget constantly with their fingers, clothing, or kick their feet when sitting. Many children with ADHD who have severe hyperactivity often play rough though they don't mean to.

ADHD causes children to act without thinking. They lack the ability to control their impulses even if they understand the consequences. A child with ADHD simply cannot think that far ahead or stop themselves to fully think about the consequences. Children with ADHD are known to constantly interrupt conversations, grab things without asking, push in line, are unable to wait for their turns, or say things that can be hurtful or rude without realizing it.

ADHD is confusing for children and many will suffer from various conditions as a result. Children with ADHD are more likely to become depressed, anxious, or have low self-esteem. They know that the behavior is unacceptable and even though they try to control themselves they cannot figure out why they are unable to do so. ADHD can look different in every child. Typically a child will be diagnosed with one of three types of ADHD:

1. Inattentive

Children with inattentive ADHD are easily distracted. They are unable to concentrate for long periods of time and have poor organizational skills. The struggles with being able to concentrate results in them missing important details, losing things, and not understanding or able to follow directions. Girls are more likely to be diagnosed with inattentive ADHD over boys. Many assume that those with inattentive ADHD are simply not listening, don't care, or are lazy.

2. Hyperactivity

Hyperactivity ADHD means the child has an excessive amount of energy. This can often be seen as the child not being able to slow down or as many describe it, the child runs on a motor. Children will often talk excessive and fidget a great deal. They will struggle to stay on task because of their need to be constantly moving. Children will constantly interrupt others when talking, be unable to wait their turn, or will act impulsively. They tend to be daredevils because they are unaware of the risk or are unable to think that far ahead to consider the dangers of their behaviors. Those with hyperactive ADHD will struggle to engage in quiet activities and need to constantly play or touch things. Boys are more often diagnosed with hyperactivity ADHD than girls. Many assume those with hyperactive ADHD are just impatient, rude, or simply do not care about consequences.

3. Combination

Combination ADHD means the child exhibits symptoms of both inattentive and hyperactivity ADHD. This is the most commonly diagnosed form of ADHD.

The symptoms your child exhibits will determine the type of ADHD they have. ADHD is a condition that your child can learn to manage but without proper treatment it can affect your child's emotions, behaviors, and can impair their ability to learn things.

Signs of ADHD

Symptoms of ADHD can be linked back to impulsivity, distractibility, hyperactivity, and impulse control. Symptoms will be present in both the home and school setting. Some of the most common signs of ADHD include:

- The child is easily distracted beyond what is considered appropriate for their age.
- The child is hyperactive.
- The child has significant impulse control issues that are not typical for their age.
- The child has exhibit inattentive and hyperactive symptoms from a young age.
- The child does not have health or learning condition that can contribute to the behaviors.

Children with ADHD are more likely to suffer from other emotional or mental conditions. This can make getting an official diagnosis of ADHD challenging. Since ADHD can be present for many years and never be addressed, other conditions can develop over that time period. By the time the behaviors of the child become a serious concern, the other issues may be more prevalent and in turn, may be the first to address. While the other conditions do need to be worked through, not addressing the ADHD can make solving the other problems impossible. If ADHD is not recognized the parent and team working will the child may be focusing on the wrong issues. It is important to know about the other conditions that can contribute to ADHD behaviors.

Common conditions that coincide with ADHD

- *Learning disabilities* - Many children with ADHD suffer from learning disabilities ranging from being unable to read letters correctly or from having really poor handwriting. Children tend to struggle to retain information or remember information and therefore struggle with test-taking.

- *Oppositional Defiant Disorder (ODD)* - This type of disorder results in the child being overly defiant and tending to ignore or challenge anything parents or adults say to them. Children with ADHD will often develop this type of disorder to try to gain control over situations. Since their thoughts and behaviors are viewed as out of control the child seeks out alternative ways to feel in control.

- *Mood disorders* - Children with ADHD have a hard time regulating their emotions. They also suffer from low-esteem which can cause them to develop depression. Because many children with ADHD are constantly being corrected, punished, or negatively viewed because of their behavior. This only adds to the poor view they have of themselves. They can easily become depressed and discouraged because, though they are trying their best to behave, remain in control, and do what is told, they cannot and they do not know why they can't. When others are constantly blaming them for not trying or not caring they feel though it is not worth putting in the effort to change the problems they are having.

- *Anxiety disorders* - Children with anxiety can become anxious and overwhelmed more easily than most other children. Anxiety and ADHD have very similar symptoms making it hard to distinguish between the two. Those with ADHD may become anxious when they have to complete a task or when they are expected to act a certain way and do not believe they are capable of.

Causes of ADHD

Despite what many believe, lack of disciple, screen time, or unstructured home life do not cause a child to develop ADHD. ADHD is the result of development and functional differences in the brain. These neurological differences can be the result of:

- Genes
- Heredity
- Prenatal alcohol or drug exposure
- Environmental toxins
- Head injuries

Though not causes for ADHD, the following can trigger or increase ADHD symptoms.

- Sugar
- Food additives and Preservative
- Too much screen time
- Diets low in omega-3s
- Lack of exercise
- Environmental toxins

Though children with ADHD suffer significantly from behavioral issues these behaviors are often the result of brain development. Cognitive abilities and key competency skills are difficult for children with ADHD to utilize and develop.

Cognitive abilities

ADHD can cause a child to struggle with various cognitive abilities. There are unable to properly sort through, store, and understand a vast majority of new information the obtain throughout the day. This is due to the fact that all the information that passes through their brain is looked at as important. At some point, they are unable to fit more information in their brain and therefore the brain needs to start deleting or removing information to make room for more. The information that is deleted is never examined or properly processed. This is why children with ADHD will often suffer from these common cognitive skills.

- *Concentration* - Children with ADHD are misunderstood in the fact that many think they are unable to concentrate on anything. Children with ADHD are in fact able to concentrate intensely on things that interest them. They can become hyper-focused on specific topics or activities. Children with ADHD tend to struggle with focusing when they are trying to focus on things that seem mundane to them. A child with ADHD needs help learning how to effectively focus their attention on all activities they take part in not just the ones that are of high interest to them.

- *Impulse control* - Impulse control is the ability to stop, think, and maintain control over our desire for something. This can be as simple as waiting your turn to speak in a conversation or not immediately touching things that are in front of you. Children with ADHD have serious impulse control issues because their brains do not allow them to quickly stop before acting out on a thought that runs through their heads.

- *Problem-solving* - Problem-solving is a skill that most children with ADHD lack. They tend to be unable to see things in steps do not fully understand cause and effect. This is why children with ADHD will often act out or have meltdowns when things are not working out the way they want.

- *Metacognition* - Metacognition refers to your child's ability to understand or even be aware of their own thoughts and thought processes. Children with ADHD have thousands of thoughts swarming their heads at any given moment. This is because they have little to no filter in what gets passed on in their brains. most people are able to quickly process and move on from one thought to another. A child with ADHD tends to have multiple thoughts passing through, which they are often unable to determine whether they are important information they should store or information that can be let go.

Competency skills

Competency skills are necessary for everyone to be able to successfully manage their life. A child with ADHD lacks a number of competency skills, which makes completing tasks and following directions nearly impossible for them. These skills are what children need to develop and learn in order to grow and be more independent. The most common competency skills children with ADHD struggle with the most include:

- *Time management* - Time management is a struggle for many children but a child with ADHD has no sense of time. In order to help a child better develop their time management, timers and schedules are essential for a child to learn and understand the importance of time management.

- *Memory* - Children with ADHD have poor short-term or working memory. This is why it is hard for them to complete any tasks that have more than three steps. Many children need to hear directions and rules repeatedly before they begin to stick in the child's memory.

- *Self-regulation* - Self-regulation refers to the emotional control you have. A child with ADHD is quickly frustrated by their emotions, which leads to extreme outbursts. Most children are highly sensitive and feel things more extremely than other children. Though highly sensitive to emotions, many ADHD sufferers are unable to identify their emotions, which causes them to respond in inappropriate ways to them.

How Can Parents Help Their ADHD Child?

The first thing you can do if you suspect your child has ADHD is to have them evaluated by a doctor. The second most important thing to do is to educate yourself. There are a number of misconceptions around ADHD and it can be challenging to understand or be patient with your child as you teach them the necessary skills they need to thrive with this condition. You may become easily frustrated when you have to constantly remind or redirect your child. You may often find yourself saying "why can you just listen?" "how many times do I have to repeat myself?" These statements can be incredibly discouraging to a child with ADHD.

Understand that your child is trying to behave in the most appropriate way but their brains are fighting against them. Children, for the most part, do not actively try to misbehave or disappoint their parents. The strategies and tips list in the last two chapters should be carefully considered and implemented if your child has ADHD. Simple lifestyle changes like eating a proper meal, getting plenty of exercises, and ensuring adequate sleep can help reduce the most common ADHD symptoms.

Chapter 9: Strategies to Increase Self-Esteem

Self-esteem is what encourages us to try new things and bounce back from disappointments. A child's self-esteem should grow as they grow and continue to increase as they develop and explore the world around them. Parents play a key role in a child's self-esteem. Paying attention, giving encouragement, and allowing a child to try something challenging helps a child feel proud and good about themselves. Many factors outside and inside the home can affect a child's self-esteem. Children who lack self-esteem may find it more difficult to control their behaviors. Low self-esteem will also lead to negative self-talk and children can grow into teenagers who make poor choices that can have a severe impact on their life.

What Is Self-Esteem

Self-esteem refers to how you feel about yourself and how you feel about what you are capable of. Having high self-esteem can help you make friends, try new things, and instill a strong, positive belief in yourself. High self-esteem is what allows you to accept and learn from your mistakes. You will be more persistent and able to find solutions to your problems to achieve the goals you set for yourself and throughout your life.

Signs your child is struggling with low self-esteem

A child that has high self-esteem is able to think positively about themselves. They know that they are liked, accepted, and believe in themselves. When a child feels good about themselves they tend to have high self-esteem. Children can suffer from low self-esteem just as teens and adults do.

When a child begins to doubt themselves, they often have a more negative view of themselves. Low self-esteem is a struggle for many children who suffer from behavioral challenges. They begin to focus on how bad they are or the mistakes they have made instead of focusing on the lessons learned or effort they put into doing something. You may notice your child is:

- Self-critical or hard on themselves
- Comparing themselves to others and expressing how they are not as good as their peers
- Only focusing on how often they have failed or messed up
- Not confident.
- Not believing they are able to accomplish things.
- Thinking they will mess up or make mistakes.

A child with low self-esteem will always question what they do and this can lead to them simply avoiding situations and people. They will struggle to make friends as they will think that others will not accept them. Low self-esteem will cause a child to give up before they even try and result in them never reaching their full potential.

Increasing Self-esteem

Self-esteem is important for children because it encourages them to learn and try new things. They develop the skills necessary to feel proud of the things they do and it can help them learn from their mistakes. Self-esteem is what will help your child try again and keep trying when things do not work out the way they originally planned. Just as with any other skills your child may require, you can build self-esteem.

They are many opportunities wherein you can increase your child's self-esteem and provide them with support to increase their self-esteem on their own. Any time your child attempts something new, learns something new, or accomplishes something on their own provides you with a perfect opportunity to give praise and let them know how proud you are of them.

There are many ways you can work with your child to help increase self-esteem from childhood to adulthood. If you notice your child may be suffering from low self-esteem, you can help them raise it so they are more confident in their abilities and like themselves more. The following are some ways you can help boost your child's self-esteem.

1. **Seek out learning opportunities.**

There are many things your child may need to learn to do on their own. Just as you help them learn to walk, feed themselves, and say the ABC's, there are plenty of new things your child can learn to help them feel more confident. Choose a new task to help your child learn such as:

- Learning to tie their shoes
- Learning to read
- Learning to write
- Learning to ride a bike
- Learning to throw a ball
- Learning to draw
- Learning to braid hair

The list can go on. Choose one task that your child either needs to learn so they can be more independent (like tying shoes), or something they would enjoy learning (like riding a bike). Set aside time each week or day to practice these new activities. This will allow your child to master vital skills as well as give you a chance to encourage and praise their hard work when they achieve the goal.

2. Allow your child to make mistakes

It can be hard to watch your child struggle when they are learning something new. Many parents want to intervene to make things easier for their child and spare them from disappointment or feeling ashamed when they make a mistake. While it is tempting to help your child avoid mistakes, these are valuable learning opportunities for a child.

You will help your child build more confidence in themselves and their capabilities when you allow them to make mistakes. You can teach them new things, show them how to do it, and then let them try for themselves. Whenever they are attempting a new skill it is perfectly fine to offer help to them but after providing them with the help of a few times you should allow them to try on their own.

When you allow your child to try something that challenges them, they can learn from the mistakes they make and feel proud for trying. A child that is able to face their challenges will be more successful as they grow into adults. You can provide your child with opportunities to face new challenges and encourage them to try even if they make a mistake. Again, remind them of how proud you are and how proud they should be of themselves.

3. Give proper praise

Praise can be a key motivation to get a child to do a number of things. Parents praise a child when they have done well in school, have cleaned their rooms, or have done something good. While praising is an effective way to encourage kids to try new things and promote positive behavior, there is a right and a wrong way for praising a child. Some things to keep in mind when you praise your child.

- *Be genuine with your praise.* If you praise your child for doing something good even when you both know it wasn't their best effort, your child will quickly pick up on the insincerity. Find another way to praise them for not giving up or being a good sport.

Do not just praise your child to praise them. Find something that will really resonate with them and allow them to feel good about the situation.

- *Focus on the effort they put into what they do.* You will want to avoid giving them praise just because of the end result, such as telling your child how great it is that they got an A. Instead focus on the effort and the skills they needed to get the results like studying hard, practicing a preferred activity like playing an instrument, to improve their skills.

- *You want to praise the progress they are making, the attitude they have as they struggle, and the dedication they exhibit.* This teaches kids to focus on the work they put towards achieving their goals as opposed to associating the end result with whether they were successful or not.

4. Be an example

Your child will automatically mimic what they see you do, so you want to ensure that you are being a good role model for your child or children. When you put effort into everyday tasks, especially those you are not enthusiastic about doing, you teach your child to put effort into the things they may not enjoy doing, but need to get done. Teaching your child to feel proud for accomplishing things like doing their homework, cleaning up after themselves, or even brushing their teeth shows them to take pride in what they do.

Keep in mind that being a good example in these situations requires having the right attitude when you are doing the tasks yourself. If you complain the whole time you are doing the dishes or folding the laundry it is more likely that your child will complain when they have to do something they don't want to do as well. Instead, maintain a positive attitude and model to your child that doing things you do want to do may not be fun but you can be proud of a job well done once you are finished.

5. Develop your child's strengths

One of the easiest ways to help your child increase their self-esteem is to focus on their strengths and the things they enjoy doing. Your child will be more eager to improve on a skill that involves an activity they enjoy and this will allow your child to see what they are capable of. If your child loves to play sports then encourage them to improve on one key aspect of the sport they love, like throwing a football further or leaning to catch a baseball. If your child has an interest in certain topics like horses, race cars, or Legos encourage them to learn more. Take them horseback riding, let the visit an indoor go-kart course, or challenge them to build a Lego city.

When you focus on your child's strengths and interests you not only show them that you are supportive of them but you teach them to pursue things they are passionate about. Allowing them to focus on the things that they enjoy and improve the skills they already possess will help them feel good about themselves.

6. Be patient

When a child hears that they are lazy, not trying hard enough, or is constantly told they can't behave, these harsh words become their internal beliefs. Many parents unknowingly give their children harsh criticism when they are acting out or not listening. This does not motivate or encourage the child to behave differently and often causes the opposite to occur. What your child hears about themselves from others is how they will begin to view themselves and eventually the way they feel about themselves will reflect the negative messages they receive.

Being patient and encouraging to your child when they are struggling or acting out in ways you don't approve of is the best way to help your child. Instead of focusing on what they aren't doing focus on what needs to be done next or what they have already done. This helps your child remain on task and reminds them that they know how to accomplish the task at hand. When your child is struggling significantly show and help them through the obstacles so they know what to do next time.

7. Acts of kindness

Helping others automatically makes you feel good and this is true for your child as well. Though it can be challenging for younger children to fully understand how acts of kindness should make them feel good, teaching them to be compassionate and considerate of others are two key skills for success later in life. When you can, perform random acts of kindness to your kids and allow them to see you doing random acts of kindness for others. This can be as simple as holding the door open for someone at the store or volunteering in the community. Teaching your child that others matter too will help them feel better about themselves when they help another person without expecting something in return. Be sure to praise your child when you notice them doing something kind for someone else, like if they pick up a cup for their sibling or shared their favorite toy.

When your child's self-esteem begins to improve, you will notice that their behavior improves as well. When your child is more confident, they feel more able to control themselves and are able to take more than just themselves into consideration.

Exercises

What are you good at?

1. Think of all the things you CAN do. Do you know how to draw? Ride a bike? Dance? Read? Write? List everything you can think of that you are good at.
2. Of all the things you listed, what is one thing, you want to get better at?
3. Think of different ways you can practice that one thing every day.

Turn your "can't" into "can"!

Trying new things can be scary and hard, at first. The voice inside your head may be telling you something is too hard, or that you *can't* do it. When you hear this voice remind yourself that can try! You can try. If you think something is too hard, remember you can always ask for help.

1. Think of some things that you want to try but have thought was too hard.

2. Who can you ask to help you learn or try this new thing with you?

3. Try the new thing.

4. How did you feel after you tried?

Chapter 10: Communication to Be Adopted With The Child

Communication is the key component to helping your child through any problems they may be having. Whether your child is suffering from anxiety, depression, anger, stress being able to listen and talk with them about what is troubling them is the first step in helping them. Communication involves knowing how to relate and understanding your child by listening to what they have to and by talking with your child to find solutions and help them overcome their problems.

Expressing Empathy

You don't have to agree with your child's behavior or why they feel a certain way, but you do want to reassure your child that you are trying to see things from their point of view. Refrain from focusing on how to fix the issues with your child. Let them know that you are there to listen and work with them through what they are struggling with. Showing your child empathy will and letting them know that you want to understand what occurred or how they are feeling is the first step in helping them identify the problem themselves.

Often times, many children are able to make the necessary adjustments to their thoughts and behaviors just by being able to express and retell their side of the situation. Remain patient and calm as your child walks you through it, and if needed help them identify the flaws in their thought patterns if they do not pick it up themselves.

For instance, if you and your child are playing a game and you win. They may immediately become upset and think they "never win" or that "it's not fair," or they may view themselves as a failure. You can listen to your child express how they are feeling in the situation and they may be able to recognize the negative thoughts and actions that coincide with how they are feeling. From there they may be able to express what they think or feel is simply untrue.

Get Down to Your Child's Level

Effective communication is a combination of speaking to your child with respect and in an age-appropriate manner as well as physically lower yourself to your child's eye-level. When you lower yourself to your child's level they will feel less intimidated and more comfortable talking to you. This also reassures your child that you are listening to what they have to say and you can more easily maintain eye contact with them.

Effective Listening

Communication is not just about how you talk to your child but also how you listen to what your child is saying to you. Throughout this book, listening has been the main component of each of the exercises and problem-solving techniques. This is because when your child feels as though you are really turned into what they are saying they feel more safe and supported. You don't have to agree with what they are saying but you do need to let them know that you hear and understand what they say.

When you listen to your child you want to give them your full attention. Maintain eye contact with your child as they speak. Looking at your phone or away from your child will indicate that you are not fully engaged in what they are saying to you. Just as you would expect your child to stop playing with toys as you are giving them a direction you want to look at your child so they know you are paying attention.

It is not always convenient or easy to stop everything you are doing to give your child your full focus. In moments like these work with your child to find a more appropriate time for the two of you to talk so that you can be completely engaged with them. Reassure them that you understand how important it is that you talk about what they want to talk about and that you want to give them your full attention when you do so.

When you are listening, you need to avoid interrupting your child. It is often difficult to listen without thinking of ways to respond to your child and this can cause you to interrupt them frequently. When you interrupt your child when they are expressing themselves you are indicating that you are not really hearing what they are trying to say. There are ways you can reassure your child that you are hearing them without saying a word. Give them an encouraging smile, head nod, or touch the arm or hand as they speak so they know you are following what they say.

Let your child know that you have heard what they have to say by restating what they have said but using slightly different words. This reassures your child that you have actually been paying attention and you can then begin to work through what is troubling them.

Encourage Your Child to Talk More

It is challenging to get some children to talk about what is going on with them. Many try to avoid these conversations because they themselves cannot make sense of what they are feeling or why they behaved the way they did. There are a number of phrases you can use to get your child to feel more comfortable about talking to you to help them through their problems. Use phrases such as:

- "I'd love to hear more about that."
- "Can you tell me more?"
- "What would you like to talk about?'
- "That sounds interesting, can you tell me more?"
- "Can you explain that to me?"
- "I am listening can you give me some more details about that?"
- "I think I understand, but can you tell me more about what happens when...?"
- "Wow! That is interesting. What happened next?"

Using phrases like these can help open the lines of communication and encourage your child to talk and explain more about what is going on with them. Keep in mind that it takes patience and practice to have effective communication occur between you and your child. Children may only be able to stay engaged in serious conversation for a short amount of time and this can make it frustrating for parents trying to help. Do not try to push your child to talk more than they are ready to talk about. Though you want to help your child, trying to pressure them to open up about their feelings when they are not ready to can cause more behavior problems and make your child feel as though you do not understand what they are experiences.

Chapter 11: Eliminating Negative Thoughts

Negative thoughts can hinder your child's ability to make friends, control behavior, and can have serious effects on your child's self-esteem, mood, and more. Children just like adults need to understand and recognize their negative thought patterns so they can learn to overcome and rewire the way their brain thinks. Changing thought patterns is not something that is quickly or easily done overnight. It takes practice. But, helping your child learn to let go of negative thoughts will allow them to let go of what holds them back. This is a skill that once they learn to master at a young age will never stop benefiting them as they grow up.

Identifying negative thought patterns with your child

1. Blaming themselves

If you notice your child is always blaming themselves for things that have happened, they are struggling with negative thinking. Children who take the blame for things in which they have had no role in the actual outcome have a negative view of themselves. They will often blame themselves for things that are the result of external circumstances which they have no control over such as a family member becoming sick. They will also over-exaggerate the severity of how things turn out even when small mistakes are made like if your child accidental spills their milk and immediately states they are the worst kid in the world.

2. Generalization

Overgeneralization occurs when your child will think the same things will always happen. If they didn't get an A on a test they will immediately think they are stupid or not smart. If they missed kicking a soccer ball, they will immediately think they will always miss and never want to play soccer again. This type of thinking stems from small obstacles that often did not turn out the way they had hoped and then becomes the foundation for their internal belief systems for things that may not even be related.

3. Easily angry

Anger is an instant reaction to a child being overly critical of themselves. If they make a mistake they will get mad at themselves quickly. This anger is their only defense mechanism when they are struggling with something and they are not able to find a solution or have formed the belief that they are unable to find a solution. If your child loses again they will lash out and not want to play anymore. They may often verbally attack the person they are playing with to release some of the negative thoughts running through their head.

4. Unwilling to try new things.

When a child thinks negatively about themselves they will often avoid trying new things. If they do not believe in their abilities to be successful at what they try, they do not bother trying. This is so they do not have to feel ashamed or face additional negative thoughts that will come from them making a mistake or not getting things right on the first try.

5. Always thinking bad things will happen.

If your child constantly looks for the negative in every situation this is a clear red flag that they need help changing their negative thought patterns. Your child will make comments that suggest that they won't have any fun, or that something always goes wrong, or that nothing good ever happens to them. This negative thinking can quickly result in them withdrawing and falling into depression.

Common negative thought patterns in children

1. Black-and-white thinking

With black-and-white thinking your child sees things as all or nothing. They or the situation is either good or bad, or successful or a failure. They look at things in one extreme or another. If something is not exactly the way they wanted, then nothing turned out the way they wanted. For example, if one child in their class didn't let them play at recess, then suddenly none of the kids or no one likes them.

2. Emotional reasoning

With emotional reasoning, your child thinks solely with their emotions and believes these emotions to be facts. A child that lets their emotions dictate their thoughts do so without looking at the whole situation or without trying to reason with how they feel. For example, your child may be afraid of a barking dog and then adopt the thinking pattern that all dogs are dangerous.

3. Overgeneralization

When your child overgeneralizes, they will focus on one small detail of a situation and use this to be their truth for all things related or unrelated to that event. For instance, if your child makes a mistake when they are coloring they will immediately think that they never do anything right.

4. Negative labeling

When your child labels themselves in a negative way they have a difficult time seeing themselves in any other way. Negative labeling is a damaging thought pattern that your child unknowing imposes on themselves and they may not be able to see themselves in any other way. For instance, your child may answer a question wrong while doing homework and jump straight to thinking, "I am so stupid."

5. Minimizing or discounting the positive

If your child is unable to see the positive or constantly discounts the positive facts of a situation they are stuck in a minimizing thought pattern. With this thought pattern you can provide your child with evidence that counters the negative view they have. They will flip this evidence or discredit it so that they still support the negative thoughts. A common example of this thought pattern would be your child tells you that a friend of theirs told them that they loved hanging around them. But, your child adds that this classmate was just saying it to be nice and that they didn't really mean it.

6. Mental filtering

Mental filtering or selective abstraction is when your child only sees the negative in themselves or a situation. They are unable to find the positives. Even if they made one small mistake they will zero in and focus just on that small detail despite any other positive feedback or experience that may have had. For example, your child may have done an exceptional job on their writing assignment but accidently reversed one of their "d's" to look like a "b." This tiny mistake becomes their focus. They don't see how well they did overall just on the small mistake and therefore, all the positive is forgotten.

Keep in mind that a certain level of negative thinking is normal and healthy. When your child has unrealistic thought patterns, however, this can cause serious effects to their emotions and the way they view the world around them. As a result, the way they behave will reflect what they think or they may act out to cope with the negative thoughts.

Explaining Negative Thoughts to Your Child

Negative thoughts can be taught to young children by explaining them using the acronym ANTs (automatic negative thoughts). When teaching young children about negative thoughts you want to help them see these thoughts as ridiculous, not that they themselves are silly for having the thought. You can help your child understand their ANTs by teaching them how to identify their ANTs.

- **A (automatic)** = The thought or phrase just pops in their head. These are uninvited and seem to push their way past everything else you may have been thinking of.
- **N (negative)** = These sudden thoughts are not very helpful or friendly. They may make you feel bad about yourself or about something that happened.
- **T (thoughts)** = These thoughts seem to be talking to you. They sound like you own little voice in your head.

ANTs can be bothersome, but you can use ANTs to explain the thought patterns your child may exhibit when they are in certain situations. You can ask them if the ANTs are bothering them. This will remind your child to stop and look at what is going on in their heads.

Once your child is able to understand and identify their ANTs they can turn them into PETs, positive effect thoughts. To do this explain PETs to your child as:

- **P (positive)** = You can use the thought to help you find solutions. You can reword the thoughts to be encouraging.
- **E (effective)** = The new thoughts should make you feel good about yourself or the situation you are in. These thoughts will help you find the truth or facts in the situation.
- **T (thoughts)** = The inner voice you are hearing is kind and helpful.

PETs are the thoughts your child can carry with them throughout the day and use them to help them through difficult situations.

Changing ANTS into PETs example:

Your child has dropped all their books while getting into the car. Their ANTs may immediately tell them:

- "I'm such a klutz!"
- "I can't do anything right!"
- "This whole day is going to be terrible!"
- "Why does this always happen to me?"

If they take a moment to pause and catch their ANTs, they can reframe what they are thinking to create PETs. Their PET thoughts can be:

- "Well, that was a silly thing to do."
- "I made a mess and can ask for help getting everything picked up."
- "This is only a small accident, the rest of my day is going to be fun!"
- "I tend to drop my stuff a lot. I can find another way to carry my stuff so it is easier for me. I can ask for help to find a better way to carry my things."

It can take time for your child to think of new and positive ways to look at themselves and the situation they are in. With practice, it will become a natural and effective way for them to overcome obstacles and work through their problems.

It is important that you do not discredit your child's thoughts or refer to them as wrong or right, good, or bad. They are simply things that need to be filtered in and out of your child's brain.

Overcoming negative thinking

Helping your child overcome their negative thoughts first begins with you being honest and taking notice of your own negative thought patterns. It is not uncommon for many parents to unknowingly pass their thought patterns onto their children. The process of identifying your own negative thoughts will benefit you and your child. Do you tend to focus on the stain you have on your shirt and think that everyone is viewing you as a messy slob? Do you tend to think negatively about how you parent just because your child is acting out or because you had to serve up frozen pizza for dinner? Recognizing your own negative thought patterns will allow you to be more understanding how your child is thinking.

Ways you can help yourself and your child overcome negative thought patterns include:

1.   Negative thoughts and accurate thoughts.

Find the facts in the situation. When a negative thought does occur, you want to pause and look at the situation in its entirety. Many times negative thoughts are easier to focus on because our brains begin to easily make assumptions about these thoughts. One way you can combat negative thinking is by putting yourself in another person's shoes. For example, your child may jump to the negative assumption that they have no friends or that no one likes them just because someone didn't say "Hi" to them. You may jump to this assumption if a friend doesn't respond to your text quickly enough.

In both instances, you can look at the situation from a different perspective. The person who did say "Hi" to your child, may not have seen her or had a really terrible morning. Just as your friend may be stuck in a meeting or their phone battery may just be dead.

You can also take the time to remember the facts about a situation. Your child may jump to the negative thought that they are stupid because they got a question wrong on a test. Focus on the facts that other questions were answered correctly.

2. Find solutions.

A lack of problem-solving skills can instantly cause a child to fall into negative thought patterns. Being able to find solutions in situations is a skill that needs to be practiced and overtime results in your child being able to overcome their obstacles with ease and accept when things simply do not work out the way they intend. Going back to the example of your child missing the question on the test. You can review the question with your child and ask them what they may not understand the question. You can also come up with a plan if your child needs to review material before a test.

You can be an example for your child when you come across something that you are struggling with. There are many opportunities that you can include your child in trying to come up with solutions for. You can have your child help you make a schedule for their day so you can get all the important tasks done and have time to spend with them. You can ask your child to help you figure out how to fit all the canned goods in the pantry.

Simple tasks that you can easily find a solution for are ideal for getting your child involved so they can develop this vital skill themselves.

It is also important that you remind your child that everyone makes mistakes and this is a part of learning.

Exercises

Create a character

It is important for children to learn and identify their negative thoughts patterns. This will help them look for the facts in the situation instead of focusing on the negativity running through their minds. A fun way you can teach your child to identify their negative thoughts is to create a character.

1. Have your child draw a character that resembles their negative thoughts.
2. Have your child give the character a name. When they begin to show signs of negative thinking you can ask if their character is having an impact on the situation. By labeling the negative thoughts in this way you give your child distance and allow them to look at things from a different perspective (the character's).
3. Once your child has created and named their character you can help your child brainstorm ways to defeat the negative thoughts. Ask your child what they can say to this character when it begins to unleash the negative thoughts

Examples:

- Your child can tell the character that it isn't the boss of them.
- Your child can tell the character that they won't listen to them because they always see things as bad and that maybe they need new glasses.

By teaching your child to identify and come up with strategies to handle their negative thinking. You are not teaching your child to ignore the negative thoughts because that doesn't help them work through or with them. Negative thoughts can be a way to show you how to look at things differently and come up with alternative solutions. Not all negative thoughts are bad as long as you can make them work with you instead of against you. By creating the character with your child you are not dismissing the thoughts, you are showing them how to look at them from the outside instead of just letting them affect them. By brainstorming ways to defeat the thoughts, you are teaching them how they can address these thoughts in a more proactive manner now and in the future.

Affirmations

Affirmations are positive phrases that you say about yourself, to yourself. Creating affirmations is an easy way for your child to not only begin to rethink what they say to themselves, it helps train the brain to think more positively. Some positive affirmations you can teach your child include:

- I am an amazing kid
- I am kind
- I am smart

- I am loved
- I am safe
- I am always helpful
- I am a good problem solver
- I am happy
- I am brave

Chapter 12: Strategies to Manage the Child's Anxiety, Stress, Depression, and Anger

There are a number of lifestyle changes that you can make to ensure that your child is physically and mentally strong. This chapter will provide you with simple ways you can encourage your child to be active, eat healthy, get enough sleep, and practice gratitude. Each of these factors can help them overcome anxiety, stress, depression, and anger.

Get Moving

One of the most effective ways to help your child manage their stress, anger, anxiety, and/or depression is with regular exercise. Exercise helps release the feel-good chemicals in the brain, so you and your child will immediately feel happier once you get yourselves moving. Exercise can also help boost your child's self-esteem and help them feel more mental strength. If your child struggles to get proper sleep incorporating a regular exercise routine can help them regulate their sleep cycle.

Exercise doesn't have to be doing 30 minutes of cardio or running around the block. Below you will find a number of ideas that can make playtime into a regular exercise time as well.

Exercise ideas for kids

1. **Create an obstacle course.**

This is one that can be done inside or outside. You can use household items you already have to create a fun obstacle course that your kids can work through. Some obstacle course ideas can be:

- Setting up a broom that lays across two chairs that your child can crawls under.
- Lining tape on the floor so that your child can jump over each line.
- Setting up small cones or coffee cans that your child can weave in and out of, like doing a soccer or football drill.
- Setting up exercise stations where they have to do 5-10 sit-ups, wall taps (where they jump up and tap the wall as high as they can), or jumping jacks.
- Have a station where they need to run in place for a minute.
- Have them use a spoon to scoop out balls or balloons from one bucket and carry them across the room to put in another bucket.

2. Races

You can set up a simple course for you and your child to race against each other. You can also include some ideas from the obstacle course to make it more fun. if the weather is nice, you and your child can create a hopscotch board and see who can get across and back first.

3. Any sport

You can play a one=on-one match of basketball with your child. You can also simply throw the football or baseball back and forth to one another. You can play tag or have them hit a few baseballs and run around the bases.

Soccer is a great sport that you can play with just you and your child. Whatever sport your child is interested in, find a way that the two of you can practice or just play in the front yard together.

4. Dance

Kids love to jump around to music, so whenever they say they are bored turn on some music and let them move around. There are also plenty of videos you can find that will allow your kids to easily learn simple steps to a song and dance along to the music.

5. Go for a walk.

Just getting outside for a quick walk can significantly improve your child's mood. If you have the opportunity to walk somewhere instead of drive take advantage of this time to get your kids outside and get in some quick exercise. If you have a dog be sure to take your kids with you when you take it for a walk or begin making it a routine to walk your dog if you don't already. You can make going on walks into a fun game of follow the leader and is a great way to get some jumping jacks, running, or other jumps in as you go.

Additionally, just allowing your child to play with a hula-hoop, frisbee, jump rope, or on a small trampoline can help them quickly get out energy and it won't feel like exercise.

Yoga

Yoga benefits your child in a number of ways. It allows them to gain control over their body, focus on their breathing, and is a highly effective way to combat anxiety and stress. Yoga can also help teach children body awareness which can help with impulse control and self-regulation.

Yoga sequence for kids

Have your child do each move for 30 seconds. After each move, have them stand up and reach for the stars. Each one has been renamed to imitate an animal making it more kid-friendly and fun!

1. Bear crawl

Have your child get on their hands and knees on the floor. Have them walk like a bear forward and back so that their knees lift off the floor and when their right hand moves up the left leg moves up to meet the left hand. Then alternate so that the left hand takes a step up and the right knee meets the right hand. Have them crawl forward a few steps then back a few steps.

2. Frog

Have your child squat down so their legs are completely bent and their hands can reach in front of them flat on the floor. This should resemble how a frog would sit on a lily pad. You can ask your child to jump up like a frog or they can simply relax in this position for 30 seconds.

3. Cat

Your child will start on the floor on their hands and knees. They should look like a tabletop where their hands are directly below the shoulders and their knees are below the hips. Ask them to arch their back up toward the ceiling as if they were a cat stretching. Then have them lower their back to their starting tabletop position. Repeat this arching of the back for 30 seconds.

4. Cow

You should have your child start in the same position as the cat pose. Instead of rounding their back to the ceiling, they will round down toward the floor and lift their head up towards the ceiling. Then they should round their back, back to their starting position. You can easily combine this pose with the cat pose so that they first round their back up to the ceiling and then immediately round their back to the floor in a smooth movement.

Maintain a Healthy Diet

What your child eats can have a serious impact on their mental health. Children who consume a diet of mostly processed foods, high sugar foods, high-fat foods, or a diet that lacks fruits and vegetables are at higher risk of developing a mental disorder and tend to have more behavioral issues.

Proper diet for kids

Your child's diet should consist of fruits, vegetables, whole grains, healthy fats, and lean proteins. Try to avoid sugary and processed snacks like chips and candy and instead allow them to have fruits, nuts, seeds, or raw vegetables.

You can make their plates more interesting by arranging their food into fun kid-friendly pictures like a butterfly, happy face, or rainbow.

Sleep

Sleep is vital for growing children and unfortunately, children who struggle with behavior issues tends to not be getting enough sleep. When a child does not get enough sleep they are more likely to have mood swings and be unable to concentrate or focus.

Recommended sleep for children

Children under the age of three should get around 12 hours at night. Children between three and 12 should get at least 10 hours of sleep.

To help promote healthy sleep patterns establish a sleep routine with your child. This can include:

- Taking a bath
- Brushing their teeth
- Setting out clothes for the next day
- Reading
- Journaling

You should keep the bedtime routine consistent and make it as calming and quiet as possible. Children should avoid watching television or having any type of screen time for at least an hour prior to bedtime.

Gratitude

Teaching children gratitude from a young age can help reduce their risk of many mental illnesses like depression and anxiety. Gratitude helps your child see all the good things they have in their life and helps them find value in themselves and the world around them. Gratitude can also teach kids empathy and to be more thankful. Starting a gratitude journal is an easy way for children to get into the habit of finding at least one thing to be grateful for each day. This is also a great activity that you and your child can do together at bedtime.

Starting a gratitude journal

Allow your child to pick out a journal that they can use for writing down what they are grateful for. Each night set aside five to ten minutes to write one to three things you are grateful for. You can prompt your child and help them find different things to be grateful for by asking them:

- What was one thing someone did nice for them today?
- What made you happy today?
- What was one thing you did really well today?
- What is your favorite toy?

- Who help you today?

Chapter 13: Exercises to Do Between Parents and Children

It is important for parents and children to work together to overcome the negative thoughts, handle emotions, and adjust behaviors together. When you work with your child through what they are struggling with, many times you will notice that you have been struggling with the same issues as well. The exercises and tools in this chapter are ideal for parent and child to do together. Each of these exercises can help your child develop the skills they need to handle their emotions, combat negative thinking, and control the way they react to overwhelming situations.

Remember to listen to your child when asking questions. It is also important to be honest and open with your child about how you may have struggled or are struggling with some of the challenges they are facing. Always provide your child with the support and love and have patience. Many of these exercises can have an immediate impact on your child's behaviors, others will need to be practiced regularly so your child can learn how to utilize the tools on their own.

Recognizing Emotions

We covered a few ways you can help your child recognize emotions such as asking them how someone feels when watching a TV show or reading a book. You can also have your child draw out the faces of each emotion and have them explain why they drew the face that way for the emotion.

Games you have around the house can be used to help your child better understand emotions as well.

Emotions Candy Land

If you have a Candy Land or the Shoots and Ladders board game you can assign an emotion or feelings to each color represented on the board (yellow for happy, red for love, purple for anger, green jealous, orange for grateful) Play as you normally would but each time they land on a color they need to tell a time when they felt that way. You can also have them say what they could have done to make someone else feel that way or have them explain what the feeling is and what activities they can do to help them feel better when they feel a certain way.

Emotions Jenga

You can buy a small Jenga set at most dollar stores instead of using a large version. Color a small circle on each block to represent a specific emotion (red for love, yellow for happy, blue for sad, purple for anger) you can use whatever colors you like and assign each an emotion. Set the game up as you normally would. Each time a block is pulled you or your child needs to tell a time they felt the emotion that corresponds with the color on the block. You can also have your child explain the emotion and ask them what they can do to help them feel better if they get a negative emotion.

Regular Jenga is a great game to help with anxiety. It can help kids become more comfortable with their anxious feelings and remind them that their anxiety is not going to hurt them. The anticipation that builds up waiting for the blocks to fall over is a key factor that can be used to help your child understand anxiety.

Indoor basketball

You can set up a simple basketball hoop using a laundry basket or clean garbage can. Crumble up a few pieces of paper to create the balls. You and your child can take turns trying to get the barber into the basket. If you get the paper in, you get two points. If you miss, you must answer a question. If you get the question right you get one point. The questions should be written out on index cards and focus on the different emotions. Some sample questions can include:

- What does it mean to feel (happy, sad, angry, worried)?
- If I am (mad, sad, worried), what is one thing I can do to feel better?
- My body feels hot and tense when I am feeling?
- When I am mad I should scream and shout. True or false?
- When I am sad I should talk to someone about what is bothering me? True or False?
- I am smiling and feel relaxed, what emotions am I experiencing?

You can include stories and ask questions about how someone is feeling, what that person can do to feel better, or what the person could have done differently to make themselves feel better.

You can set a goal to reach for how many points you need to acquire before the game is over. For younger children, you might want to say the first person to get to 5 or 10 points wins or for older children 20 points or more.

Breathing techniques

Teaching your child a number of breathing techniques can help them instantly calm their body and thoughts when they are confronting something they fear. These breathing techniques help slow down the heart rate and allow your child to gain control over their emotions. They can be used in any setting and should be practiced frequently, not just when your child is feeling a certain unpleasant emotion.

- Starfish breathing

Have your child stand with their arms stretched out to their sides. Have them take a deep breath as they reach their arms up above their heads. As they exhale, have them bring their arms back down to their sides.

- Blowing bubbles

You can provide your child with actual bubbles to blow or have them pretend to blow bubbles from an imaginary wand. Have them practice taking a deep breath in so that the air fills up their bellies, then have them slowly exhale. If you are using actually bubbles you can tell them that the slower the exhale the breath the bigger their bubble will be. Then have them pop the bubbles as they think about the negative thoughts or emotions they are experienced as a way to release the negativity from their minds.

- Counting

You can have your child inhale for a count of five and then exhale for a count of five. You can also have them hold their hands out in front of them and use their opposite pointer finger to trace the outline of the fingers o. Each time they run their finger up the side of the opposite hand they should inhale, when they run their finger down the side of the finger on the opposite hand they should exhale.

Impulse Control

There are a number of games you can play that will teach your child impulse control without them even knowing. When you are done playing these games you can ask your child how they were able to stop when they needed to or how they were able to follow directions. Then use what they have said to relate to how they can do this in their daily activities.

Red Light, Yellow Light, Green Light.

This is a simple game that can be played indoors or outdoors. You can position yourself at one end of the room or across from your child. When you say green light your child can move forward to try to "tag" you, when you say yellow light your child must slow down, and when you say red light your child must stop. Your child cannot move again until you say green light.

Simon Says

Simon says is a common children's game where one person is Simon and the other must do what "Simon Says" each direct must be started with

"Simon Says" (Simon says touch your nose, Simon says hop on one foot, Simon says stop hopping on one foot). If the direction does not start with Simon says, then the child should not do as directed, if they do then the game is over and you can start again.

Freeze Music

This is a fun way to get your child moving and help with impulse control. Play music for your child to dance around to, when the music stops your child must freeze in whatever position they are in. When the music starts again your child can begin to dance again.

Mindfulness

Mindfulness teaches your kids to get in tune with their body, focus on breathing, or become more aware of their surroundings. There are a number of ways you can incorporate mindfulness into your daily lives. Ways to practice mindfulness throughout the day:

- You can teach mindfulness when you go on a walk. As you and your child walk ask them questions about what they feel physically (like the wind blowing on their face), hear, see, and smell. Then ask them how each of these sensations make them feel.
- You can practice mindfulness when you eat with your child by asking them how what they eat tastes and how they think the food helps their body stay healthy and strong.

- You can help your child become more mindful of what they are thinking by asking them what is going on in their heads. Ask them how their thoughts are making them feel. If they are thinking something negative, ask them how they can reword what they are thinking so they feel better.

Journaling

We covered starting a gratitude journal in the previous chapter but journaling to get thoughts and events of the day out of your child's head is a good, general activity to practice. Journaling can help your child work through difficult problems, help them celebrate their victories from the day, and can help them track the progress they are making. You don't have to have a journal set for a specific reason. You can simply ask your child to write about their day, something that interests them, or something that may be bothering them. They can also just write whatever thoughts run through their mind for a set amount of time. If your child struggles to get into the habit of journaling you can have some prompts handy for them to write about.

Journal prompt ideas:

- Who is one person you look up to?
- What would you love to do with your best friend if you knew you would be told No?
- Where is one place you would like to go?

- What was your favorite thing about the weekend?

- What is your favorite subject in school?

- What is a subject you wished you could learn more about in school?

- What is your favorite food?

- Would you rather play a sport or play an instrument? Why?

- What is your favorite season? Why?

- What is your favorite color? How does that color make you feel?

- What is one act of kindness you did for someone else today?

- What is something you want to learn to do?

- What is your favorite cartoon character? If you could spend a day with this character what would you do?

Conclusion

When your child is acting out, they are ultimately trying to tell you that something is hard for them to work through on their own. While you may not want to admit or believe that your sweet child is suffering from intense emotions like depression, anxiety, or trauma, it is not uncommon for children to experience these things. You may have tried everything you could think of to help your child change their behavior without understanding what the root cause was.

This book has provided you with the information that allows you to understand why your child is acting out and what thoughts and emotions they are struggling with. You have to learn how to identify red flags and how you can begin to help your child understand and overcome their struggles.

Throughout this book, you have gained valuable tools and techniques commonly used through Cognitive Behavioral Therapy. You can begin to utilize these tools today to help your child understand how their thoughts, emotions, and behaviors are all connected. You are encouraged to practice the techniques and use the activities on a daily basis so your child can gain the control they desperately want over themselves.

As you assist your child through their struggles, remember to remain calm, patient, and understanding. These big emotions are a struggle for many adults to overcome, just imagine how much your child is struggling. With the information provided in this book, you can help your child overcome the biggest problems and strengthen the skills necessary to be successful in all areas of their life.

References

Angry Kids: Dealing With Explosive Behavior. (n.d.). Retrieved from https://childmind.org/article/angry-kids-dealing-with-explosive-behavior/

Department of Health & Human Services. (2011, December 31). Trauma and children – tips for parents. Retrieved from https://www.betterhealth.vic.gov.au/health/healthyliving/trauma-and-children-tips-for-parents

Dowshen, S. (Ed.). (2015, February). Childhood Stress (for Parents) - Nemours KidsHealth. Retrieved from https://kidshealth.org/en/parents/stress.html

Garey, J., Claire, M., Nyu, New York Times, Los Angeles Times, & American Library Association. (n.d.). How to Change Negative Thinking Patterns. Retrieved from https://childmind.org/article/how-to-change-negative-thinking-patterns/

Khanna, A. (2019, July 24). Want your child to be Active, Fit & Healthy? Retrieved from https://flintobox.com/blog/child-development/exercise-games-kids

Lyness, D. A. (Ed.). (2018, July). Your Child's Self-Esteem (for Parents) - Nemours KidsHealth. Retrieved from https://kidshealth.org/en/parents/self-esteem.html

Lyness, D. A. (Ed.). (2018, October). Anxiety Disorders (for Parents) - Nemours KidsHealth. Retrieved from https://kidshealth.org/en/parents/anxiety-disorders.html?WT.ac=ctg

Matheis, L. (2019, October 4). Signs Of Anxiety In Children: Child Anxiety Symptoms. Retrieved from https://www.anxiety.org/causes-and-symptoms-of-anxiety-in-children

Wright, L. W. (2019, October 16). Signs of Anxiety in Young Kids. Retrieved from https://www.understood.org/en/friends-feelings/managing-feelings/stress-anxiety/signs-your-young-child-might-be-struggling-with-anxiety

CPSIA information can be obtained
at www.ICGtesting.com
Printed in the USA
LVHW050712090421
683977LV00015B/509

9 781801 127837